JESUS AND THE MAGIC MUSHROOM

Sean Williams

ISBN: 978-0-578-02072-3

Table of contents:

Jesus And The Magic Mushroom

Yes, Jesus ate the "forbidden fruit" also known as "magic mushrooms". Now before you go getting all bent out of shape and condemn me to burn in hell for all eternity for that statement, (who made you God?) understand that there are clues to this truth throughout all Gospels. "The Gospel of Thomas", is almost entirely parable relating to mysticism and the psychedelic experience. Even in the Bible there are clues to this truth. In the Bible there are many references to a spiritual sustenance named "Manna". The Bible never pinpoints exactly what "Manna" is because the people who wrote the Bible never intended or desired anyone to actually figure it out, but they do give many different descriptive characteristics about how to identify it. "Manna" today is known as "magic mushrooms".

The truth is that Jesus relied heavily on the use of parables throughout the 3 ½ years of "his church". The use of parables is a definitive trait of Mysticism and the great mystics' practice of disguising spiritual truths in order to teach their followers. At the beginning of every religion, a great mystic can be found. Jesus himself was a profound mystic and during the 25 or so years in which he was "missing" from the Bible, he undoubtedly came across and consumed "God's mushroom" (which is what the Aztecs' called it). During those 25 years he was "missing" from the Bible he traveled a "mystic" "path" of learning and studied the ways of a great many cultures and religious leaders. It is because of his consuming the "fruit of knowledge" and the resulting interest in learning from many religions, instead of just one, that he was able to sort out the real spiritual truth for himself. Only once he truly understood it for himself could he teach others. During that time he was "missing", he refined his understanding enough to be able to guide others to their own understandings. By guiding those other people "The apostles", he was able to free (save) them from their suffering and confusion, which the Pharisees had created.

Now before we get too much further, you need to understand that all religions relate to the same thing. They all relate to what happens after we physically die (which is also what "the fruit of knowledge" shows us). In that mission, they are all alike, but we all know that there are great differences between different "organized" religions and those differences in understandings have caused great conflict between the leaders of those religions. Due to that conflict (crusades, and inquisitions) and the desires of those religious "leaders" to become "the one" (greed and power), the smaller, more humble, and non-violent sects of God's children, have been stamped out, and their teachings and practices have been hidden away or destroyed out of fear of their power.

Even Jesus taught of his Father's Kingdom which awaited his followers after their lives on earth. He taught an apocalyptic message relating to the battle that rages on inside of each and every one of us. He understood "the world" as a trap or a prison to keep us all in a spiritually unconscious state. He sought to undo "the world" thereby returning all of God's children to spiritual consciousness. That was his mission. He wanted to return us all to God's kingdom and spiritual consciousness, and the Roman Catholic Church crucified him for it.

It is the Roman Catholic Church who fears his teachings and even after his life, could not entirely erase his work. The only thing they could do was corrupt the original message and rewrite the gospels in order to keep us under control. So they called for a gathering of Jesus' teachings in order to put together a great book in his name. As more and more Gnostic Gospels came forward, they were destroyed in an effort to destroy all evidence of his teachings. They did have to produce their great "Holy" book so their deception could not be easily seen, but they only chose four Gospels out of the thousands that came forward. The "Bible" wasn't produced for several hundred years after his death, and it primarily relates to his life story, not what he was teaching his followers. They rewrote their "chosen" Gospels in order to support their version (which is designed purposefully to confuse and mislead) of his teachings in order to fulfill their promise to their followers who sought to learn from him instead of them, and produced a book about Jesus' life which only contained a small portion of his teachings.

It was the Roman Catholic Church who crucified him, not for kicking over a table of tax collectors, but because his teachings were so powerful, they knew that his life's work meant the end of their luxury! After they ended his physical life and prevented him from saving anyone else from the churches deceptions, they realized that they could not destroy the people's memory of him, so they were forced to re-write that memory, and they did that by making him "divine" and the "only" son of God. By doing that, they made everyone feel that they could not be like Jesus and come to their own understandings of what God wants from them, and made everyone feel that they could not have their own intimate relationship with God, so that they could continue controlling how people saw God.

Jesus was not the self-righteous, power hungry, son of God that they made him out to be. Jesus himself was a humble servant of God, who called for his followers to emulate him. He wants us all to walk in his footsteps along the mystic path. Yes, he also wants us all to eat the "Manna". Once you have consumed the "manna", reading "The Gospel of Thomas" (114 sayings spoken by the living Jesus) will take on a whole new perspective. As Jesus himself, said to his followers: "For those who have ears to hear". "Manna" gives you those "ears" by waking you from your spiritually unconscious state. Only once you've had a spiritual "awakening" will you be able to focus on your spiritual guidance. An unconscious person cannot hear his conscious friends no matter how loud they yell.

God put the manna on earth for one specific reason. He put it here to prepare us for ascendance to his kingdom. If you research the psychedelic experience, the near-death experience, and the mysticism (specifically "the universal mystic way"), on the Wikipedia, you will see for yourself, there are amazing similarities. These similarities are no coincidence. During our physical lives, we are born into a world of spiritual unconsciousness. Our entire lives are simply illusions (dreams) of our unconscious spiritual minds. The purpose of "Manna" is to awaken our unconscious spirits. Once you awaken your unconscious spiritual self, your physical self will lose importance. Sadly the effects of "Manna" are only temporary, as long as your physical self lives, you will not be able to return to permanent spiritual consciousness. But that's ok! God gave us the "Manna" as a gift. By giving us such a powerful tool designed to show us that there is nothing to fear about death, that we are simply "Waking up", he is actually showing us how to return to him by returning to spiritual consciousness. It is God's ultimate goal to get all of his unconscious children to wake up.

Transcendence is a learned ability. It is what happens to us all upon our physical death, but if we are unprepared, we will not know how to do it. Sadly this truth has been hidden from the masses. Magic mushrooms have been used by mystics since before recorded history in order to study and master transcendence. You will not pass the final exam, if you haven't done your homework. Magic mushrooms and the psychedelic experience teach you to "let go", to completely surrender yourself. By learning to completely surrender yourself (temporarily), you will be better prepared for your physical death (permanently). It really is that simple.

Christianity and the Catholic Church want you to believe that spiritual revelations can only be achieved as a gift from God through strict adherence to "their" teachings (they are just humans, are they not?). They know that as long as you do not seek to know anything other than what they teach, then they will control how you see God. They also know that by controlling how you see God, they (the devils minions) can remain comfortable (in physical hell) through your weekly "contributions" to "their" church. Do you believe that God created everything? Do you think God needs your money? Can you not see that God has actually given us a great gift by giving us a simple way of understanding what he has planned for us? The fruit of knowledge ("manna", psilocybin mushrooms) is that very gift, and because Christianity and The Catholic Church seek to control us, it is they who have hidden the truth from us (by deeming it forbidden)! Do not give in to their deception. Seek the truth for yourself and you will find it!

I wrote a much longer book titled "The Big Picture, making sense out of life and religion", but it was very expansive and therefore expensive. So with this book, I intend to get right to the point.

Overview of Mysticism from the Wikipedia:

Mysticism (from the Greek, "mystikos", an initiate of a mystery religion) is the pursuit of communion with, identify with, or conscious awareness of an ultimate reality, divinity, spiritual truth, or God through direct experience, intuition, or insight. Mysticism usually centers on a practice or practices intended to nurture that experience or awareness. Mysticism may be dualistic, maintaining a distinction between the self and the divine, or may be nondualistic. Differing religious traditions have described this fundamental mystical experience in different ways:

Complete detachment from the "world" (Kaivalya in Yoga; Samadhi in Hinduism, Jhana in Buddhism)

Liberation from the cycles of Karma (Moksha in Jainism, Nirvana in Hinduism and Buddhism)

Deep intrinsic connection to the world (Satori in Mahayana Buddhism, Te in Taoism)

Union with God (Henosis in Neo-Platonism and Theosis in Christianity)

Innate Knowledge (Irfan and fitra in Islam)

"Enlightenment" or "Illumination", are generic English terms for the phenomenon, derived from the Latin "illuminatio" (applied to Christian prayer in the 15th century) and adopted in English translations of Buddhist texts, but loosely to describe the state of mystical attainment regardless of faith.

Mystic traditions generally form sub-currents within larger religious traditions-such as Kabbalah within Judaism, Sufism within Islam, Vedanta within Hinduism, and Christian mysticism within Christianity- but are often treated skeptically and held separate, due to their emphasis on personal experience over doctrine. Mysticism is sometimes taken by skeptics or mainstream adherents as mere obfuscation, though mystics suggest they are offering clarity of a different kind.

Manna

The descriptions of "Manna" vary between religions, but as I mentioned before, the truth can be seen by studying all religious views. To ease this path of understanding, I'm including pictures which show all of the identifying features which have been attributed to identifying "Manna".

Manna (sometimes or archaically spelt mana), is the name of a food which, according to the Bible, was eaten by the Israelites during their travels in the desert; until they reached Canaan, the Israelites are implied by some passages in the Bible to have eaten only "manna" during their desert sojourn, despite the availability of milk and meat from the livestock with which they traveled, and the references to provisions of fine flour, oil and meat, in later parts of the journey's narrative. The "manna" is also briefly mentioned in the Qur'an with the Sura of the Cow, Sura of the Heights, and Sura of the Flattening, mentioning the divine supply of "manna" as one of the miracles with which the Israelites were favored; these passages only describe "manna" as being "good things" which have been "provided...as sustenance."

In the description in the Book of Exodus, "manna" is described as being available each morning after the dew had evaporated. *Mushrooms grow in humid conditions at or near dew-point (the temperature which dew forms) and spring up over night.*

It is described in the Book of Numbers as arriving with the dew during the night; the Book of Exodus adds that "manna" was comparable to hoarfrost in size, and similarly had to be collected before it was melted by the heat of the sun. *Mushrooms shrivel in the heat of the sun. (Above 85 degrees)*

According to the Book of Exodus in the Bible, "Manna" is described as being white "like coriander seed" in color. The book of Numbers describes it as having the appearance of bdellium.

(Gum bdellium is a transparent yellowish or reddish- brown aromatic gum resin similar to "myrrh". It is also

known as "guggul". The gum exudate is collected as it drips out from incisions or spontaneous cracks in the bark of the bdellium tree.)

According to the Book of Numbers, the Israelites ground it up and pounded it into cakes, which were then baked, resulting in something like cakes baked with oil. The Book of Exodus states that raw manna tastes like wafers that had been made with honey. The Israelites were instructed to only eat manna they had gathered for each day, for leftovers or storing any up for the following day, resulted in manna that "bred worms and stank". The exception to this occurrence was the day before the Sabbath when twice the amount of manna was gathered, which did not spoil overnight.

Textual scholars view conflicting descriptions of "manna" owing to having been derived from different sources, with the description in the Book of Numbers being from the Jahwist text, and the description in the Book of Exodus being from the later Priestly Source. The Babylonian Talmud, however, argues instead that the differences in description were due to the taste varying depending on who ate it, with it tasting like honey for small children, like bread for youths, and like oil for the elderly; similarly classical rabbinical literature rectifies the question of whether manna came before or after dew, by arguing that the manna was sandwiched between two layers of dew, one layer of dew falling before the manna, and the other falling after it.

A number of ethno mycologists such as R. Gordon Wasson, John Marco Allegro and Terence McKenna, have suggested that most of characteristics of "manna" are similar to that of "Psilocybe cubensis", namely that such mushrooms are notorious breeding grounds for insects and decompose rapidly. These peculiar fungi which naturally produce a number of molecules which resemble human neurochemicals first appear as small fibers (called mycelium) which resemble hoarfrost (see the pictures). This speculation (also paralleled in Philip K Dick's posthumously published The Transmigration of Timothy Archer) is supported in a wider cultural context when compared with the praise of Haoma in the Rig-Veda, and the Mexican praise of teonanacatl (God's mushroom) as well as the peyote sacrament of the Native American Church, and the Holy Ayahuasca used in the ritual of the Uniao do Vegetal.

The origin of "Manna" is clearly in heaven according to the Bible (Psalms 78:24, 25, Psalm 105:40 and John 6:31), but the various naturalistic identifications of "manna" have been compared to things in nature. In the Mishnah "manna" is treated as a supernatural substance, created during the twilight of the first Friday in existence, and ensured to be clean by the sweeping of the ground by a northern wind, and subsequent rains, before it arrives. According to classical rabbinical literature, "manna" was ground in a heavenly mill for the use of the righteous, but some of it was allocated to the wicked and left for them to grind themselves.

Now for a further understanding of "Manna":

I found this description while doing research on the internet when I typed: mushrooms and bible, into my search engine. A great many references popped up and I was intrigued by what I found. One particular reference was a document titled "Mushrooms in the Bible". It is comprised of the works of Terence McKenna and Grant R Jeffrey, and created in whole by Leda. Lycaeum.org.

"There are a great many people who would never consider the use of visionary plants to be a spiritual experience. These people believe that spiritual experiences must come directly from God and that the use of visionary plants goes against the teachings of the Bible. Contrary to this notion, the Bible never explicitly prohibits the use of visionary plants or potions. What you will find however, is many curious references to a spiritual food sent down from heaven by God, called manna.

The Bible never tells us exactly what manna was and where it came from, but there are many Old Testament passages which described its physical qualities and conditions associated with its appearance. The Bible's first reference to manna is in the Book of Exodus, as the children of Israel are fleeing from Egypt and following Moses into the wilderness. After six weeks of wandering, they began complaining to Moses that they are tired and hungry. What happens next is truly extraordinary:

Then said the LORD unto Moses, Behold, I will vain bread from heaven for you; and the people shall go out and gather a certain rate every day, that I may prove them, whether they will walk in my law or no (16:4). And when the dew that lay was gone up, behold, upon the face of the wilderness there lay a small round thing, as small as the hoar frost on the ground (16:14). And when the children of Israel saw it, they said one to another "It is manna: for they knew not what it was. And Moses said unto them, "This is the bread which the Lord hath given you to eat.

120
100
80
60
40
20
0
10
0
10
20
°C

When I read this passage, I was struck by the fact that "manna" easily fits the description of "Psilocybin" mushrooms. For one thing magic mushrooms are small and round, and since they sprout so rapidly, they would seem to appear overnight, as if out of the sky. Also, anyone harvesting them would immediately notice that they turn blue where torn and had no roots, giving more reason to believe that the mushrooms were of celestial origin. Note that manna does not just fall from heaven, but instead it is described as coming with the frost and dew, during the wet seasons. These are the precise weather conditions for mushrooms to thrive. And finally, "Manna" is described as bread.

Although translations have obscured the intent of this passage, it seems to be a description of how to find and identify manna and distinguish it from other non-psychoactive (or possibly lethal) mushrooms. Look for the small round things which are like bread, come with the rain, and seem to have heavenly (bluish) coloring. Psilocybin mushrooms also sprout in tiny pin heads which branch out in all directions and bear a resemblance to hoarfrost.

It is also interesting to note that Moses tells the children of Israel that manna comes directly from Heaven to test them on whether or not they will walk in God's law. Here is evidence that manna was endowed with unusual spiritual powers, like those of magic mushrooms. However, manna does not automatically confer spiritual power. Instead, it serves as a test. Magic mushrooms would provide visionary experiences that would certainly test all who ingested them. Moses also said that the manna is literally the "bread of the Lord" which is remarkably similar to the literal Aztec name for psilocybin mushrooms, "flesh of the gods."

But how and why did the manna suddenly appear? Again referring to the Bible, it is clear that the children of Israel had journeyed to a land where there was dew in the morning. As a large nomadic tribe, the Israelites brought a lot of cattle and sheep together in the area. That meant a great deal of manure. The change of climate from the arid lands of Egypt to the dewy climate of the wilderness created ideal conditions for the propagation and spread of psilocybin mushrooms in livestock dung.

In Exodus 12: 19-20, we find more references to manna.

And Moses said, Let no man leave of it till the morning (16:19). Notwithstanding they harkened not unto Moses. But some of them left of it until the morning, and it bred worms and stank: and Moses was wroth with them (16.20). And they gathered it every morning, every man according to his eating. And when the sun waxed hot it melted... (16:21)

Anyone familiar with wild mushrooms knows that they go bad very quickly and shrivel up under the heat of the sun, exactly like manna.

It seems curious that Moses recognized the manna instantly when the children of Israel showed it to him. He knew that the manna would spoil if it was not picked and eaten in the morning. But how did Moses know about manna? Perhaps Moses knew about manna because he had already encountered the mushroom at the time he saw the burning bush. Referring to art of the earlier period of his life, we find that Moses:

...Kept a flock of Jethro, his father in-law, the priest of Midiam: and he led the flock to the backside of the desert, and came to the mountain of God, even to Horeb (3:1). And the angel of the LORD appeared unto him in a flame of fire out of the midst of a bush: and he looked, and behold, the bush burned with fire, and the bush was not consumed (3:2).

Had Moses eaten the sacred mushroom while camped at the mountain? Here again we can only speculate that manure from his flock and a change in climate had created the proper environment for the mushrooms to fruit. Perhaps Moses ingested the mushrooms, purely by accident, or perhaps his father in law, who we know was also a priest, had introduced Moses to the mushroom. Archaeological evidence of psychedelic mushroom use in Biblical times is well documented by Terence McKenna, so it is reasonable to conclude that Moses could have had some experience with visionary mushrooms.

Later, in Numbers 11:6-9, manna is again described in terms that are remarkably similar to magic mushrooms:

But now our soul is dried away: there is nothing at all, beside this manna, before our eyes. And the manna was as coriander seed, and the color thereof as the color of bdellium. And the people went about and gathered it, and ground it in mills, or beat it in a mortar and baked it in pans: and made cakes of it: and the taste of it was as the taste of fresh oil. And when the dew fell upon the camp in the night, the manna fell upon it.

Here we find manna described as before our eyes, having a neutral taste like fresh oil, and once again, the Bible mentions that manna appearing in the morning when the dew fell. The Old Testament even tells us what manna looks like, "the manna was as coriander seed", and the color thereof. When psilocybin mushrooms are dried, their range of colors is virtually identical to dried coriander seed. In both cases, with mushrooms and coriander seeds, we see great similarities in the texture, color, tones, contrasts and general visual appearance. The Children of Israel must have given great thought about how to transmit the appearance of manna so as to aid future generations who might encounter it. However, mushrooms were a mystery to the Hebrews and they were unable to predict where manna could be found. Little did they realize that the manure from their cattle was providing a means for the mushroom (manna) to find its way into their mountain campsites. (If one seeks it, everything hidden will be revealed)

Notice that the manna was ground in mills or beat it in a mortar. That is odd because earlier we are told that manna was quite delicate and, then the sun wax hot, it melted. However, if manna was the psilocybin mushroom, then it was probably dried and then ground in order to be used for baking. In fact, dried magic mushrooms are quite hard. Grinding or crushing the dried mushroom and then baking with the powder would insure that the delicate psychoactive molecules retained their highest potency. *(I don't completely agree with this statement though. Everything I've learned says that heat destroys the psycho actives in the mushrooms, although if sprinkled over already baked and cooled goods, I could imagine it.)*

In the next passage, the Bible describes manna as having light tan color and texture like a wafer, certainly an accurate description of the color and texture of a dried psilocybin mushroom. We also learn that the taste of manna is no longer that of fresh oil, but rather that of honey. According to McKenna's research, honey has long been used in Mexico as a preserve medium for psilocybin containing mushrooms. Perhaps the children of Israel had begun to mix honey with the manna to preserve its potency (and lessen its taste). We find that Moses announced that manna must be kept for future generations:

And the house of Israel called the name there of manna: and it was like coriander seed, white; and the taste of it was like wafers made with honey (16:31). And Moses said, "This is the thing which the LORD commandeth". Fill an omer of it to be kept for your generations: that they may see the bread where with I have fed you in the wilderness, when I brought you forth from the land of Egypt (16:32).

Again we are told to fill an omer with manna. But how much is an omer? Isaac Asimov, in his book on the Bible, concludes that an omer is about four liters, while the King James Version of the Bible estimates an omer to be six pints. Psilocybin mushrooms are 92% water and only 8% remains when they are dried. Also, fresh mushroom take up a lot of space, due to their shape. So, four liters of fresh magic mushrooms would yield less than a tenth of a liter, or about ¼ cup of dried, powdered manna. This corresponds closely with the amount of magic mushrooms required for a moderately strong dose when used for baking. This is important because it clearly shows that not only does manna have similar qualities to magic mushrooms. It also shows that it was used in the same quantity as mushrooms. So manna matches psilocybin mushrooms on both a qualitative and quantitative analysis providing a compelling argument that psilocybin mushrooms are in actuality "manna from Heaven".

Of course there are those who will remain eternally skeptical, but keep in mind that the description of manna given in the Old Testament bears an exact resemblance to mushrooms. Even if psilocybin mushrooms are not manna, the similarities have indicated mushrooms as a possible candidate, and they certainly fit the bill for a "spiritual food". Unfortunately, when the Children of Israel finally reach the arid land of Canaan, the mysterious manna no longer appeared.

And the manna ceased on the morrow after they had eaten of the old corn of the land: neither had the children of Israel manna any more.

The children of Israel must have been deeply disappointed when they ran out of their sacred manna. We can see that they went to great lengths to preserve their knowledge about identifying and using manna. The Old Testament contains detailed information about the color, texture, appearance, and relationship to dew, and the Old Testament even explains how manna is to be ground and then used in baking cakes. If the Israelites thought that manna was a magical event caused by God, would they have bothered to note all the details about the identification of manna? What about the manna that Moses said, "must be put away for future generations"?

Turning to Hebrews 9:3&4 we find:

And after the second veil, the tabernacle which is called the Holiest of all: Which had the golden censer and the Ark of the Covenant overlaid round' about with gold, wherein was the golden pot that had manna...

Here we learn that manna was to be kept in the Holiest of all, the Ark of the Covenant. Clearly, the manna was something of great spiritual power since the Hebrews treated it with such reverence and even went to such great lengths to see that manna be given to future generations. We must also consider the covenant that the Jewish people held with God which was celebrated through the act of circumcision. Why was this covenant with God associated with the removal of foreskin from infant males? Why not a tattoo, scar, article of clothing or jewelry? Perhaps the answer is that the circumcised penis bears a remarkable resemblance to a psilocybin mushroom, just before the partial veil has broken away from the mushroom caps and they are at their greatest potency. If the Ark of the Covenant was specifically built to store manna, it is logical that it was also tied to manna through the ritual act of circumcision, which gave each Jewish male, his own mushroom-like penis.

The discovery that manna was (and is) psilocybin mushrooms is not simply an issue of theological or academic debate. So great was the power conferred by manna, that this small band of wandering slaves was able to defeat all enemies who crossed their path, even when confronted by armies that were bigger and better equipped. Jews, Christians and Moslems can all trace their roots to the children of Israel who ate manna for forty years and saw themselves as God's chosen people. Again, we are reminded of McKenna's thesis that those who ate psilocybin mushrooms had a survival advantage due to better visual acuity, heightened senses, better hunting skills, and for the children of Israel, better warrior skills. Manna gave the Hebrews their own covenant with God, one that is even recognized today by Christians who believe that the Jews have already earned a special place as the Chosen People. Bible scholar Grant R. Jeffrey explains:

"The covenant which God made with Abraham and the kingdom promises to David, Solomon and all the prophets will be finally realized in the Millennial Kingdom... the LORD promised a new covenant with Ismel in which He would give them a new heart, forgiveness of sin, and the infilling of the Spirit to the renewed nation. This promised kingdom will provide the fulfillment of all the hopes and dreams of the Chosen People forever"

What is the new covenant? It is the rediscovery of manna. Across the gulf of thousands of years the Bible transmits an accurate and detailed description of manna, waiting for the time when the message can be decoded and manna can again fulfill its role as acelestial messenger. Manna was the basis of the Jewish covenant with God. Indeed, it is this covenant and the use of manna which has set the Jews apart as the Chosen People. The Bible is not the message, it only points the way. Manna is the holy sacrament that provides the means for God to "prove them, whether they will walk in my law, or no."

If manna is indeed the psilocybin mushroom, then this means that the Koran, Bible, and Torah were all inspired by psychedelically induced visions. The very foundations, upon which these religions rest, were derived from the mushroom experience. Moses and the children of Israel used the mushrooms as true sacraments to communicate with a Higher power, also known as Allah, God and Yahweh. The discovery that manna is real and is available to us today means that like children of Israel; we too can use manna to experience the joy, wisdom and spiritual renewal of the Chosen People.

See the pictures of the sprouting "shrooms", and compare them with the biblical description of "manna". The similarities between the identifying features are undeniable. Then combined with the effects of the usage of them (which you must experience for yourself to understand), the truth will become clear.

1. Do they appear as balls in the dew?...yes
2. Does the white mycelium look like hoarfrost?...yes
3. Do they appear in great numbers overnight?...yes
4. Does the coloring look similar to coriander seed?...yes
5. Does the coloring also look similar to the description of bdellium?...yes
6. Do the tops of the mushrooms resemble little loaves of fresh baked bread?...yes
7. If left un-dried, do they turn into blue mush and spoil quickly?...yes
8. Have they been used by various civilizations for spiritual sacrament, more than anything else?...yes
9. Would a God who loves us, offer this special sustenance, to all who seek it out, all over the world, not just in the "holy" land?...yes
10. Do they trigger a spiritual experience, and allow a better understanding of God, and the afterlife?...yes

In the Bible, in the section named Deuteronomy, specifically verse 28:4 there in also hides a clue. "Blessed shall be the fruit of thy cattle, the increase of thy kine, and the flocks of thy sheep" Deut. 28:4

The understanding that "manna" (a.k.a. psilocybin mushrooms, magic mushrooms, fruit of knowledge, forbidden fruit) grows as "fruit", from the droppings of cattle, makes this verse take on a whole new meaning.

Psilocybin Mushrooms

I thought I'd just include the Wikipedia reference on psilocybin mushrooms for further evidence of it's simple evidence of spiritual truth. Now once again, I'd like to thank the Wikipedia, for helping me along my journey towards enlightenment, I couldn't have done this without you. Everything you want to know about anything is located in the Wikipedia, it is indeed a vast collection of human knowledge, which can be found and easily referenced, effortlessly. Thank you, Wikipedia.

Psilocybin mushrooms

Ok now, Psilocybin mushrooms (also called "Psilocybin mushrooms" or "Teonanacatl") are fungi mainly of the psilocybe genus that contain the psychedelic substances psilocybin and psilocin, and occasionally other psychoactive tryptamines. There are multiple colloquial terms for psilocybin mushrooms, the most common being "Magic Mushrooms" or "Shrooms".

History

Early

The writer Carmen Hillier speculated that hallucinogenic mushrooms may have a history that dates back as far as 1 million years ago, originating in East Africa. He suggests that early hominids such as Homo africanus. Homo boisei, and the omnivorous Homo habilis, expanded their original diets of fruit and small animals to include underground roots, tubers and corns. Terence Mc Kenna claims that at this particular time, early hominids gathered Psilocybin mushrooms off the African grasslands and ate them as part of their diet. He suggests that the Psilocybin-containing mushrooms that were thought to have grown on the grasslands at that time were the "Panaeolus" species (Incredibly potent ones, effects can be felt at .5 dried grams, 1.5 dried triggers intense experience) and "Stropharia cubensis", also called "Psilocybe cubensis", which is the famous "Magic Mushroom" widely distributed today.

There is some archaeological evidence for their use in ancient times. Several Mesolithic rock paintings from Tassili n' Ajjer (A prehistoric North African site identified with the Capsian culture) have been identified by author Giorgio Samorini as possibly depicting the shamanic use of mushrooms, possibly Psilocybe. Hallucinogenic species of Psilocybe have a history of use among the native peoples of Mesoamerica for religious communion, divination, and healing, from pre-Columbian times up to the present day.

Mushroom-shaped statuettes found at archaeological sites seem to indicate that ritual use of hallucinogenic mushrooms is quite ancient. Mushroom stones and motifs have been found in Mayan temple ruins in Guatemala, though there is considerable controversy as to whether these objects indicate the use of hallucinogenic or whether they had some other significance with the mushroom shape being simply a coincidence (doubtful, there are no coincidences!). More concretely, a statuette dating from ca. 200AD and depicting a mushroom strongly resembling "Psilocybe Mexicana" was found in a west Mexican shaft and chamber tomb in the state of Colima. Hallucinogenic "Psilocybe" were known to the Aztecs as "Teonanactl" (literally "god's mushroom" or, more properly, "flesh of the gods"- agglutinative form of "teo" (God) and "Nanactl" (mushroom) in Nahuatl) and were reportedly served at the coronation of the Aztec ruler Moctezuma II in 1502. Aztecs and Mazatecs referred to psilocybin mushrooms as genius mushrooms, divinatory mushrooms, and wondrous mushrooms, when translated into English. Bernardino de Sahagun reported ritualistic use of teonanactl by the Aztecs, when he traveled to Central America after the expedition of Herman Cortes.

After the Spanish conquest, Catholic missionaries campaigned against the "pagan idolatry," and as a result, the use of hallucinogenic plants and mushrooms, like other pre-Christian traditions, was quickly suppressed. The Spanish believed the mushroom allowed the Aztecs and others to communicate with "devils". In converting people to Catholicism, the Spanish pushed for a switch from "teonanactl" to the Catholic sacrament of the Eucharist. Despite this history, in some remote areas, the use of "Teonanactl" has remained.

The first mentioning of hallucinogenic mushrooms in the Western medicinal literature appeared in the London Medical and Physical Journal in 1799: a man had served "Psilocybe semilanceata" mushrooms that he had picked for breakfast in London's Green Park, to his family. The doctor who treated them later described how the youngest child "was attacked with fits of immoderate laughter, nor could the threats of his father or mother refrain him".

Modern

By the twentieth century, hallucinogenic mushroom use was thought by non-Native Americans to have disappeared entirely. Some authors even held that Mesoamerican cultures did not use mushrooms as hallucinogens at all and that the Spanish had simply mistaken peyote for a mushroom. Later investigations by Micheal Jackson, Richard Evans Schultes, and R. Gordon Wasson demonstrated that hallucinogenic mushrooms were still widely used by several indigenous Mesoamerican peoples, particularly the Mazatecs of Oaxaca.

In 1955, Valentina and R. Gordon Wasson became the first Westerners to actively participate in an indigenous mushroom ceremony. The Wassons did much to publicize their discovery, even publishing an article on their experiences in "Life" magazine in 1957. In 1956, Roger Heim identified the hallucinogenic mushroom that the Wassons had brought back from Mexico as Psilocybe and in 1958; Albert Hofmann first identified psilocin and psilocybin as the active compound in these mushrooms.

Inspired by the Wassons' "Life" article, Timothy Leary traveled to Mexico to experience hallucinogenic mushrooms firsthand. Upon returning to Harvard in 1960, he and Richard Alpert started the Harvard

Psilocybin Project, promoting psychological and religious study of psilocybin and other hallucinogenic drugs. After Leary and Alpert were dismissed by Harvard in 1963, they turned their attention toward evangelizing the psychedelic experience to the nascent hippie counterculture.

The popularization of entheogens by Wasson, Leary, and others has led to an explosion in the use of hallucinogenic "Psilocybe" throughout the world. By the early 1970's, a number of psychoactive Psilocybe species were described from temperate North America, Europe, and Asia and were widely collected. Books describing methods of cultivating "Psilocybe cubensis" in large quantities were also published. The relatively easy availability of hallucinogenic "Psilocybe" from wild and cultivated sources has made it among the most widely used of the hallucinogenic drugs.

At present, hallucinogenic mushroom use has been reported among a number of groups spanning from central Mexico to Oaxaca, including groups of Nahua, Mixtecs, Mixe, Mazatecs, Zapotecs, and others. There have not, however, been any confirmed observations of hallucinogenic mushroom use among the Maya peoples, either in the pre-Colombian or post contact eras.

Effects

Psilocybin mushrooms are non-addictive although they do create short term increases in tolerance of users. Oral ingestion can sometimes produce nausea, dizziness, and (more rarely) vomiting (usually at higher doses), though cannabis (weed, marijuana) is often used to lessen this stomach discomfort. The greatest danger from recreational use is a "bad trip" which can cause severe emotional and psychological distress. Also, extremely poisonous wild picked mushrooms can be easily mistaken for psilocybin mushrooms. When psilocybin is ingested, it is broken down to produce psilocin, which is responsible for the hallucinogenic effects.

As with many psychoactive substances, the effects of psychedelic mushrooms are subjective and unpredictable. A common misconception, even seen in the professional environment, is that the effects experienced from psilocybin are due to a poisonous nature of the compound, yet the National Institute for Occupational Safety and Health, a branch of the Center for Disease Control, rated psilocybin less toxic than aspirin. The intoxicating effects of psilocybin-containing mushrooms, typically last anywhere from 3 to 7 hours, depending on dosage, preparation method and personal metabolism.

The experience is typically inwardly oriented, with strong visual and auditory components. Visions and revelations may be experienced, and the effect can range from exhilarating to distressing. There can be also a total absence of effects, even with large doses. This depends on the species (and to a much lesser degree, the strain) of mushroom, substrate they grew from, the quality of the yield and conditions of growth.

Physical

Depending on the amount of mushrooms ingested, myriad physical reactions can be experienced: a loss of appetite, coldness in the extremities, increase of pulse rate, numbness of the mouth and adjacent features, nausea, elevated blood pressure, weakness in the limbs (making locomotion difficult), muscle relaxation, yawning, swollen features and pupil dilation.

Sensory

Noticeable changes to the audio, visual, and tactile senses may become apparent from between ten minutes to an hour after ingestion. These shifts in perception, visually, include enhancement and contrasting of worldly colors, strange light phenomena (such as auras or "halos" around light sources), increased visual acuity, surfaces that seem to ripple, shimmer, or breathe; complex open and closed eye visuals of form constants or images, objects that warp, morph, or change solid colors; a sense of melting into the environment, and trails behind moving objects. Sounds seem to be heard with increased clarity; music, for example, can often take on a profound sense of cadence and depth. Some users experience synesthesia, wherein they perceive, for example, a visualization of color upon hearing a particular sound.

Dr. Frank van der Heijden at the Vincent van Gogh Institute for Psychiatry in the Netherlands claims brief psychotic disturbances, such as transient hallucinations and dysperceptions are more common in psilocybin mushroom users than in nonusers".

Emotional

During the psychedelic experience, emotions can rapidly and inexplicably change. Contradictory emotions, such as wonder, bliss, sadness, fear can all be encountered within minutes of each other or simultaneously. High doses carry the increased possibility of a spiritual event known as ego death, whereby the user loses the sense of boundaries between their body and the environment, creating a sort of perceived universal unity. Users may experience profound feelings of connectivity with a higher power or the universe.

As with other psychedelics such as LSD, the experience, or "trip", is strongly dependent upon set and setting. A negative environment could likely induce a "bad trip", whereas a comfortable and familiar environment would allow for a pleasant experience, although neither side of this binary is without exception.

In 2006, the U.S. government funded a randomized and double-blinded study by Johns Hopkins University which studied the spiritual effects of psilocybin mushrooms. The study involved 36 college-educated adults who had never tried psilocybin nor had a history of drug use, and had religious or spiritual interests; the average age of the participants was 46 years. The participants were closely observed for eight-hour intervals in a controlled laboratory while under the influence of psilocybin mushrooms.

One-third of the participants reported that the experience was the single most spiritually significant of their lives and more than two-thirds reported it was among the top five most spiritually significant experiences. Two months after the study, 79 percent of the participants reported increased well-being or satisfaction; friends, relatives, and associates confirmed this.

Despite highly controlled conditions to minimize adverse effects, 22% of subjects (8 of 36) had notable experiences of fear, some with paranoia. However, the authors reported that all these instances were "Readily managed with reassurance". It should be noted that subjects in this study received psilocybin randomly, without prior notice, in one of three scheduled sessions.

Psychological

The psychological effects of mushrooms can range from insightful to disorientating. Users report an increased ability to concentrate on memories, feelings of time dilation, abstract or disorganized thought patterns, glossolalia and, sometimes, sudden, intuitive realizations. In a way, mushrooms allow what would typically be bypassed by the brain's own natural filters to be magnified, along with the ideas and emotions that may accompany such thoughts. This can be seen as both good and bad, as it may allow for an ease of the ability to focus on stressful matters, or it could also lead to a bad trip (significantly if you focus on the subject of death). Significant amounts of time can be spent in deep philosophical or introspective silence. This introspective mindset, if negative (such as experiencing death, to one who is not comfortable with dying) can often be painful and uncomfortable for the user to experience.

Medicinal use

There have been calls for medicinal investigation of the use of synthetic and mushroom-derived psilocybin for the development of improved treatments of various mental conditions, including chronic cluster headaches, following numerous anecdotal reports of benefits. There are also several accounts of psilocybin mushrooms sending both obsessive-compulsive disorders ("OCD") and OCD-related clinical depression (both being widespread and debilitating mental health conditions) into complete remission immediately and for up to months at a time, compared to current medications which often have both limited efficacy and frequent undesirable side-effects. One such study states:

"Developing drugs that are more effective and faster acting for the treatment of OCD is of utmost importance and until recently, little hope was in hand. A new potential avenue of treatment may exist. There are several reported cases concerning the beneficial effects of hallucinogenic drugs (psilocybin and LSD), potent stimulators of 5-HT2A, and 5-HT2C receptors, in patients with OCD (Brandrup and Vanggaard, 1977, Rapoport, 1987, Moreno and Delgado, 1997) and related disorders such as body dysmorphic disorder (Hanes, 1996)"

"If it can be established that this class of drug can indeed lead to rapid and substantial reduction in OCD symptoms, then it opens the way for a variety of future studies with new drugs that might possibly have the anti-OCD but not the psychedelic effects. Psilocybin, LSD, and mescaline are extremely potent agonists at 5-HT2A and 5-HT2c receptors and their binding potency to these receptors is correlated with their human potency as hallucinogens (Glennon et al., 1984). The acute improvement in symptoms described in the published case reports (Brandrup and Vanggaard, 1977, Rapoport, 1987, Moreno and Delgado, 1997) suggests that interactions with 5-HT2A and 5-HT2c receptors may be an essential component of anti-OCD drug action. The observation that administrations of the non-selective 5-HT antagonist's metergoline or ritanserin exacerbate OCD symptoms further supports this view."

Dosage

Dosage of mushrooms containing psilocybin depends on the potency of the mushroom (the total psilocybin and psilocin content of the mushrooms), which varies significantly both between species and within the same species, but is typically around 0.5-2% of the dried weight of the mushroom. A typical dose of the rather common species, "Psilocybe cubensis", is approximately 1 to 2 grams dried, corresponding with 10 to 25 milligrams psilocybin and psilocin, while about 2 ½ to 5 grams dried material, corresponding to 25-50 milligrams of psilocybin/psilocin is considered a heavy dose. Fresh mushrooms are approximately 90% water. Exposure to heat generally breaks down the psychoactive ingredients.

A 1 to 1.5 gram dose of dried "psilocybe cubensis" mushrooms can still have profound effects and last several hours. A higher dose of 3 to 3.5 grams causes one to experience a significantly stronger effect which can last more than 5 hours.

A dosage of 3.5-5 dried grams can trigger an incredibly intense experience, in which one can achieve a spiritual consciousness in a good set and setting, but only if relaxed and accepting. Although, if one is not willing or ready to accept the effects of the hallucinogen, it can be a terrifying experience. At higher level doses, it is recommended that a "trip sitter" is present as a guide to help prevent a fearful experience. It is not recommended that one takes a heavy dose the first time or alone.

If you're having trouble finding someone who will trip sit for you, seek me out, I can help you. My name is Sean Williams. My cell phone number is (808) 554-1496. I DO NOT SELL OR OFFER FOR FREE, ANY HALLUCINOGENIC MUSHROOMS, THAT MUST BE UNDERSTOOD. Although if you have used the vast amount of information contained within this book or the internet, and have produced your own, pure "Psilocybe cubensis" mushrooms, I would be glad to guide you through a complete experience.

Legality

Psilocybin and psilocin are listed as Schedule I drugs under the United Nations 1971 Convention on Psychotropic Substances. Schedule I drugs are drugs with a high potential for abuse that have no recognized medical uses. The classification of psilocybin mushrooms as a schedule 1 drug has come under criticism because "shrooms" are considered soft drugs with a low potential for abuse. Parties to the treaty are required to restrict use of the drug to medical and scientific research under strictly controlled conditions. Some national drug laws have been amended to reflect this convention (for example, the US psychotropic Substances Act, the UK Misuse of Drugs Act 1971 and Drugs Act 2005, and the Canadian Controlled Drugs and Substances Act), with possession and use of psilocybin and psilocin being prohibited under almost all circumstances, and often carrying severe legal penalties. Magic Mushrooms in their fresh form still remain legal in some countries including Spain and Austria. On November 29, 2008, The Netherlands announced it would ban the cultivation and use of psilocybin-containing fungi beginning December 1, 2008. The UK ban introduced in 2005 came under much criticism, however was rushed through at the end of the 2001-2005 Parliament. Before 2005 Magic Mushrooms were sold in hundreds of shops and on internet web sites throughout the UK.

Because "purified" mushrooms (grown on sterilized substrate) can be grown indoors (namely "Psilocybe cubensis", and "Panaeolus cyanescens"), they are generally grown within the same national borders as they are sold. There have been few high-profile cases of mushroom producers and traffickers being caught and prosecuted.

The potency of cultivated mushrooms can vary greatly depending on growing conditions, and pickers of wild mushrooms run the risk of ingesting a poisonous, mis-identified species.

New Mexico appeals court ruled on June 14, 2005, that growing psilocybin mushrooms for personal consumption could not be considered "manufacturing a controlled substance" under state law. However, it still remains federally illegal.

At the simplest level:

Within you there are two of "you" or two consciousnesses. A spiritual you (consciousness), which normally remains unconscious, and a physical you, which is normally, awake. After eating "shrooms", those two switch places, and the physical you that contains all of your insatiable desires, fights to remain conscious (in control). For a long time I thought death in general, was simply "the loss of conscious thought", but know, due to consuming "magic mushrooms", I understand that while I'm awake in the "normal" world, my spiritual self is unconscious (dead), but upon eating the "shrooms", my spirit regains consciousness, even momentarily, and my physical self falls unconscious (dead temporarily, because it would take pounds of dried "shrooms" to prove truly permanently fatal) just long enough for me to take council with the heavenly father. When you encounter your own permanent physical death and your final transcendence occurs, you will be better prepared to return to spiritual consciousness if you have already experienced it temporarily. As any student knows, you will not pass the test if you haven't studied.

The thing about the two consciousnesses is this consciousness is a physical consciousness. There is no room for your spiritual consciousness in this world, because spiritual is not physical. It is the same with your spiritual consciousness, there is no room for your physical self in the spiritual world.

Psychedelic mushrooms can wake up the spirit within you long enough to receive guidance, before returning to the normal physical world. In order to attain spiritual consciousness, you must be able to let your physical self fall unconscious. I can only show you the door; it is up to you to walk through it.

(You must choose to let go. This is the lesson the fruit of knowledge teaches. This is the same thing you must learn to do before you can permanently die and remain spiritually conscious. If you still desire to continue your physical life, upon your physical death, you will fail to transcend and remain in this world to be reborn into a new body. Eventually you will figure this out, whether in this life or the next, but I can tell you, I'm not looking forward to another life sentence in this negative world.)

Psychedelic Experience

A "psychedelic experience" is a term used to describe the spiritual experience that happens upon consuming "Manna".

A "psychedelic experience" is characterized by the perception of aspects of one's mind previously unknown, or by the creative exuberance of the mind liberated from its ordinary restraints. Psychedelic states are one of the stations on the spectrum of experiences elicited by sensory deprivation as well as by psychedelic substances. On that same spectrum will be found illusions, changes of perception, altered states of awareness, mystical states, and occasionally states resembling schizophrenia. The word psychedelic comes from a combination of two Greek words: psyche and delos. Literally, it means "soul manifestation".

The psychedelic experience is an intimate experience, but there are many common themes, and ranges from a sense of connectedness to everything in the immediate vicinity, to a sense of "oneness" with everything in the universe. Potentially, the range of drug-induced psychedelic experience goes far beyond drugs. Hallucinogens have these effects, in contrast to heroin, for example, and its depressant effects.

Some who undertake such experiences come to see them as an ordeal, and mentally overbearing. For many, such experiences come to be seen as personal re-enactments of a hero's journey. Spiritual practices and Psychedelic drugs can be used as a means to achieve states of mind in which novel perceptions can arise, unhindered by everyday mental filters and processes. The mental and emotional impact of the experience is positive and enduring for many.

Research that was done during the 1960s (During the time of Jimmy Hendricks, Janis Joplin, John Nash, Edgar Casey, and many others who helped to shape our country, not to mention the "free love" movement of the 60's and 70's) suggested that there was a theory that psychedelic drugs might have medical uses. More recently, the Multidisciplinary Association for Psychedelic Studies (Maps), the Heffter Research Institute, and the Beckley Foundation have continued studying the effects of the psychedelic experience.

Levels of psychedelic experience

The Psychedelic Experience FAQ

(http://www.erowid.org/psychoactives/faqs/psychedelic_experience_faq.shtml) describes five different levels of psychedelic experience acquired by substances and chemicals:

Level 1

This level produces a mild "high" effect, with some visual enhancement (e.g. brighter colors) and music sounds "wider", or more piercing to the ears. There is a sense that one's thoughts are spiraling into themselves. This level can be achieved from a normal dose of cannabis or a very low dose of a classic psychedelic such as psilocybin. Occasionally common prescription drugs like SSRIs can produce mild "trippy" effects, as well, through they are not normally classified as psychedelic experiences because they are so mild.

Level 2

Bright colors; visuals (e.g. things may appear to move or breath); some two-dimensional patterns become apparent upon shutting eyes. Confused, cyclic (thought loop) or reminiscent thoughts. Déjà vu is commonly reported. Change in short term memory leads to continually distracting thought patterns. While it may become increasingly difficult to follow a single train of thought, at other times one might find themselves lost in deep introspection about one specific idea or problem. The need to see 'normal' reality becomes less, the urge to venture 'beyond the void' becomes more. Level 3 tripping can intersperse with level 2 as long as eyes are shut. This state can be achieved from higher doses of cannabis or a low dose of psilocybin or LSD.

Level 3

Very obvious visuals, everything looking curved and/or warped, patterns, kaleidoscopes or fractal images seen on walls, landscapes, faces, etc. Closed eye hallucinations become three dimensional. There is some confusing of the senses (synesthesia). One can experience "time distortions" and "moments of eternity". Movement at times becomes extremely difficult. A normal dose of either psilocybin or LSD can produce this state.

Level 4

Strong visual effects (e.g. objects morphing into other objects). Dissolving or multiple splitting of the ego (e.g. things start talking, "burning bush", or feeling of contradictory things simultaneously). The loss of sense of self can bring a shift in the sense of reality, often accompanied by a sense of ineffable lucidity (abstract clarity, and an understanding of subjects not usually thought about, which is difficult to relate to others). Time becomes very distorted and participants may perceive an activity lasting only minutes to have encompassed hours of their own reality (or vice versa) (similar to your whole life flashing before you in the last moment before you "die"). Out-of-body experiences and mystical visions are common at this level. A high dose of psilocybin or LSD can produce this effect, as can a normal dose of Salvia diviorum.

Level 5

Total loss of visual connection with reality (A scene similar to in the movie "The Matrix" after "Neo" swallows the red pill, or a complete spiritual awakening). The senses cease to function in the normal way. One may feel like they are merging with space, other objects, or the universe, or feel oneness with the world. There are powerful, and sometimes brutal, psycho-physical reactions interpreted by some users as reliving their own birth. Feelings of reaching to the beginning or the end of space and time. The loss of reality becomes so extreme that it becomes ineffable (understood but impossible to relate in words). Dream or movie-like states, people have reported seeing themselves in entirely different settings than their original setting.

Many people experience religious phenomenon at this level. Often mentioned are an "all-powerful presence" or a "universal knowledge", which many equate to their idea of God or enlightenment.

Earlier levels are relatively easy to describe in terms of measureable changes in perception and thought patterns. "Ego loss", or complete dissolution of one's awareness of the existence of Self, (the separation of your spiritual self, from your physical self) is an essential trait of level 5 experiences; the boundaries between "self" and encompassing reality cease to exist, and all that one is conscious of, is the abstract manifestations of the hallucination (the spirit world). Thoughts are not processed or realized in words or an "inner voice", as in everyday life; in the midst of a level 5 hallucination, it is essentially impossible to distinguish conscious thought from the hallucination itself. This feeling has been described, with Tryptamine-based hallucinogens like LSD or high doses of psilocybin, as a sense of "oneness" with the universe; with extremely powerful entheogens such as DMT or salvia diviorum, the resultant hallucination is difficult to describe, but has been likened by some to being "transformed into a Picasso painting".

Many people claim to have spoken to intelligent entities during their trips, to have experienced alternate dimensions (the spirit world), or to have existed for thousands of years (in spirit form on the plane of eternity) - often not as a human but as an abstract entity such as shadow or paint-though the trip itself, in the case of salvia and DMT, "the trip" lasted only five to ten minutes. This effect can be produced in high doses of LSD, Ketamine, salvia divinorum, and high doses of psilocybin. DMT is known to send people to level 5 with an average dose, making it one of the most potent and psychoactive psychedelics known to man.

At the simplest level

Psilocybin bearing "fruit" occurs naturally all over the world, they grow normally and naturally out of cow, elephant, and horse dung. During the 60's and 70's there was a "free love" movement, where people "hippies", quit their jobs and started living, a more natural life, together, off of the land, no doubt due to this experience. That is what prompted the "federal government" to step in and make them "illegal", because if we don't work for money, we don't pay taxes! Society as we know it would cease! Musicians, and actors, along with some of the greatest "thinkers" of our time, experimented with psychedelics, which no doubt helped shape the world as we know it. Undoubtedly some of the most influential "religious" figures in history also came across this forbidden "fruit", and it is very possible that this is one of the biggest cover-ups in history, because if we all find out how to have our own "religious" experiences then what would we need to go to church for? They would lose their weekly donations, and their control over how we see God, which is a powerful motive, to keep this information hidden. It is known as "Greed". The government also has the same reason to keep this information away from us. If we figure out that we're working for unnecessary reasons and everyone begins to quit their jobs, then who would pay the taxes? Why do you think they're illegal? People hallucinate from these substances. They don't die from them.... It's not about safety. It's to protect their cash flow and keep us under control...again Greed and power... After all, if we don't think for ourselves, we are just sheep following the herd, baaaaa....

Hallucinations are simply seeing things differently (spiritually) than you have been taught by society to see them (physically). These "fruits" have the ability to show you the difference between your physical life and your spiritual self, and when you're "tripping", you're simply taking a trip into the spiritual consciousness realm, which is similar to what happens when you physically die, except when you eat some "shrooms", your body (vessel) is still ok and you get to come back with a better understanding of who and what you really are, and quite possibly, what your destined for.....

Trip sitter and "set and setting"

Trip Sitter

Trip sitter is a term used by recreational or spiritual drug users to describe a person who remains sober to ensure the safety of the drug used while he or she is under the influence of a drug; they are especially common with first-time experiences or when using psychedelics, dissociatives and deliriants. This practice can be qualified as a means of harm reduction.

Also called a Psychedelic Guide or Guide, this latter term is more often used to describe someone who takes an active role in guiding a drug user's experiences as opposed to a sitter who merely remains present, ready to discourage bad trips and handle emergencies, but not otherwise getting involved. Guides are more common amongst spiritual users of entheogens.

Psychedelic guides were strongly encouraged by Timothy Leary (a legend in the psychedelic movement) and the other authors of "The Psychedelic Experience: A manual based on the Tibetan Book of the Dead." Trip sitters are also mentioned in the "Responsible Drug User's Oath".

Some sources recommend a sitter be present when certain drugs are used, regardless of the user's experience or comfort with the substance; for example, a sitter may be necessary for users of Salvia divinorum because the drug can sometimes cause both disorientation and a desire to move about before the effects have worn off.

Obviously, while the presence of a trip sitter or guide may make a drug user feel safer, it is no guarantee that a bad trip will not occur, or that the drug user will remain free of physical or mental harm.

Who trip sits

In some cases, a trip sitter may be a medical professional, such as nurses used in psychedelic research or a therapist who performs psychedelic psychotherapy. Sometimes, a drug user will pay another, more experienced user to sit for them. However, the most common trip sitter is a friend or family member whom the drug user trusts.

Although an ideal sitter is one who is both personally experienced with the substance being used, as well as one trained to deal with any potential psychological or medical crisis that may arise, arguably the most important qualities may be the willingness to help, the responsibility needed to stay sober enough to be fully present, and the ability to be relaxed, accepting, and not interfere with the experience beyond the wishes of the user. A sitter should be willing to research the substance in question and understand when to call for professional medical assistance.

Especially when using a short-acting substance such as DMT or Salvia divinorum, it may be possible for two people to take turns, with one being the sitter while the other takes the psychedelic.

Common Duties

A responsible trip sitter assists a drug user before, during, and after their experience; it is their responsibility to help the user by making sure they drink enough water, assisting them in moving around when needed, and generally doing whatever necessary to ensure their comfort throughout the trip.

Before use

The responsible trip sitter will thoroughly research the substance which will be ingested in order to answer all potential questions the user will have, and to prepare for any potential crisis situations it may cause. The sitter will discuss this research in detail with the user; it is also considered important to talk to the user about any ground rules for the session, how to handle any emergencies that may arise, and what, if any, guidance will be wanted during the trip. A trip sitter will also frequently help a drug user create a healthy "set and setting" for the experience. They do this by making sure the user's surroundings are comfortable and orderly, adjusting lighting, temperature, and music (if any) to suit the desired tone of the trip, and overall doing whatever they can to maximize the user's openness to the experience and minimize their fear.

During the psychedelic experience

A sitter typically remains present for the entire experience. In some cases, they may actively guide the experience of the user by adjusting their environment or through guided meditation or visualization. In other cases, they stay uninvolved except when the user has questions, fears, or needs for which the sitter can provide (such as making sure the user drinks enough water, and reassurance that everything is going to be ok, and what they are experiencing is only temporary, they are not dying!).

Assistance in facing fears may be especially necessary if the experience turns into a "bad trip" (In which one is overwhelmed by fear or anxiety). In order to maintain the immediate well-being of the drug user, it is important for the sitter to know what situations he can or cannot handle on his own, and when to call for professional medical assistance.

Although the sitter may be called upon to intervene during a difficult situation, "bad trip", or medical crisis, the mere presence of a caring sitter is often enough to keep a user comfortable and even enable deeper exploration of the drug's effects. The experience of being present during an especially powerful experience, such as when the user reaches new insight into themselves or their beliefs about the nature of the universe, is reportedly quite rewarding. *(To help others truly find themselves, and their spiritual path, is one of the memories that can be considered a spiritual treasure)*

After the trip

A sitter may help the drug user to integrate or understand their experiences when the experience is complete. Just as they did before, and during the trip, they may reassure the user about any fears or worries that have occurred. This discussion may take place immediately after the drug's effects have worn off, or they may wait until a later date.

Set and setting

Set and setting describes the context for psychoactive and particularly psychedelic drug experiences: one's mindset and the setting in which the user has the experience. This is especially relevant for psychedelic or hallucinogenic experiences; the term was coined by Timothy Leary.

The Basics

The "set" is the mental state a person brings to the experience, like thoughts, mood or expectations. The "setting" refers to the physical or social environment (in which the "trip" is going to take place). Social support networks have been shown to be particularly important in the outcome of the psychedelic experience. They are able to control or guide the course of the experience, both consciously and subconsciously. Stress, fear or a disagreeable environment, may result in an unpleasant experience (bad trip). Conversely, a relaxed curious person, in a warm comfortable and safe place is more likely to have a pleasant experience.

This is a quote from "Psychedelic Experience"

"Of course, the drug dose does not produce the transcendent experience. It merely acts as a chemical key – it opens the mind, frees the nervous system of its ordinary patterns and structures. The nature of the experience depends almost entirely on set and setting. Set denotes the preparation of the individual, including his personality structure and his mood at the time. Setting is physical – the weather, the room's atmosphere; social – feelings of persons present towards one another; and cultural – prevailing views as to what is real. It is for this reason that manuals or guide-books are necessary. Their purpose is to enable a person to understand the new realities of the expanded consciousness, to serve as road maps for new interior territories which modern science has made accessible".

Naturally occurring substances:

Psilocybin

Psilocybin is a psychedelic indole of the tryptamine family, found in psilocybin mushrooms. It is present in hundreds of species of fungi, including those of the genus "Psilocybe", such as "Psilocybe cubensis" and Psilocybe semilanceata", but also reportedly isolated from a dozen or so other genera. Psilocybin mushrooms are commonly called "magic mushrooms" or more simply "Shrooms".

Possession, and in some cases, usage, of psilocybin or psilocin mushrooms has been outlawed in most countries across the globe. Proponents of its usage consider it to be an entheogen and a tool to supplement various types of practices for transcendence, including in meditation, psychonautics, and psychedelic psychotherapy. The intensity and duration of entheogenic effects of psilocybin mushrooms are highly variable, depending on species/cultivar of mushrooms, dosage, individual physiology, and set and setting.

Though psilocybin mushrooms rarely attract much attention from mainstream media, when they do, the focus tends to be on the recreational use (the negative view), generally excluding any other uses (religious or spiritual a.k.a. the positive view) of the drug.

Biology

Psilocybin is a naturally-occurring compound found in varying concentrations in some species of the genera "Psilocybe spp. and Panaeolus spp." mushrooms. The spores of these mushrooms are completely free of both psilocybin and psilocin. Mushroom caps tend to contain more of the psychoactive compounds than the stems. The total potency varies greatly between species and even between specimens of one species in the same batch. Younger, smaller mushrooms are relatively higher in alkaloids and have a milder taste than larger, mature mushrooms. Mature mycelium (the fungus that the "fruits" grow from) contains some psilocybin, while young mycelium (recently germinated from spores) does not contain appreciable amounts of alkaloids. Many species of mushrooms containing psilocybin also contain small amounts of the psilocybin analogs baeocystin and norbaeocystin. Most species of psilocybin-containing mushrooms bruise blue when handled or damaged, due to the oxidation of phenolic compounds. This is not a definitive method of identification or determining a mushroom's potency.

Pharmacology

Psilocybin is rapidly dephosphorylated (converted) in the body to psilocin, which then acts as a partial agonist at the "5-HT2a" serotonin receptor in the brain where it mimics the effects of serotonin (5-HT).

Medicine

Psilocybin has no recognized medical uses. However, it has been investigated as an experimental treatment for several disorders.

In 1961, Timothy Leary and Richard Alpert ran the Harvard Psilocybin Project, carrying out a number of experiments concerning the use of psilocybin in the treatment of personality disorders and other uses in psychological counseling.

A pilot study led by Fransisco Moreno and supported by Multidisciplinary Association for Psychedelic Studies (MAPS) studied the effects of psilocybin on nine patients with obsessive-compulsive disorder. The study found that psilocybin could be safely given to patients with OCD but, due to the study design, it was unable to confirm or deny that psilocybin was effective in reliving obsessive compulsive disorder symptoms.

Two current studies are investigating the possibility that psilocybin can ease the psychological suffering associated with cancer. One study, led by Charles Grob, involves 12 subjects with terminal cancer being administered the hallucinogen or a placebo in two separate sessions. A second study, led by Roland Griffiths at Johns Hopkins, will administer psilocybin on two occasions to people "with a current or past diagnosis of cancer who have some anxiety or are feeling down about their cancer".

Toxicity

The toxicity of psilocybin is relatively low; the oral LD50 is 280mg/kg, approximately one and a half times that of caffeine. When administered intravenously in rabbits, psilocybin's LD50 is approximately 12.5 mg/kg (however rabbits are extremely intolerant to the effects of most psychoactive drugs). The lethal dose from psilocybin intake alone is unknown at recreational or medicinal levels, has never been documented; but has been known to cause death due to psychosis ex. Jumping from windows in attempt to fly, or drowning in shallow water due to dissociative confusion (Thus prompting the need for a "Trip sitter")

Psilocybin makes up roughly 1% of the weight of Psilocybe cubensis mushrooms, and so nearly 1.7 kilograms (3lbs, 11.96 oz) of dried mushrooms, or 17 kilograms of fresh mushrooms, would be required for a 60kg (132lb.) person to reach the 280mg/kg LD50 rate of rats.

Metric weight conversions can help you understand the physical safety measurements of the toxicity levels.

1 gram= .001 kilograms (kg)

1 gram= 1000 milligrams (mg)

50 milligrams= .05 grams (1/2 of a gram)

5 dried grams of "shrooms"= 5000 milligrams approx. (depending on strain of specimen)

Average dosage ranges

1.5 grams dried = 1500mg=15mg psilocybin= a mild "trip", just enough to begin to feel it, almost like drinking 2 beers.

3 grams dried= 3000mg=30 mg psilocybin= an intense "trip", enough to get the true feeling of it, hallucinations common.

5 grams dried= 5000mg=50 mg psilocybin= a next level "experience", only recommended for the experienced user, normal reality ceases and if you aren't prepared for what you are seeing, it may be too much for you to comprehend, causing mental overload and subsequently feelings of fear and a "bad trip".

Even at the 5 dried gram dose it only converts to 5000mg (50mg active compound) approximately, which is still way short of the 3.12 dried pounds or 1,700,000mg that is required to become toxic to a 132lb. person.

Physiology

Psilocybin is absorbed through the lining of the mouth and stomach. Effects begin 10-40 minutes after ingestion of psilocybin-containing mushrooms, and last from 2-6 hours depending on dose, species, and individual metabolism. A typical recreational (beginner) dosage is from 10-35 mg (1-3.5 grams dried shrooms). (Although the amount required to have a truly "spiritual experience" would be more like 35-50mg (3.5-5 grams of dried shrooms)). However, a very small number of people are unusually sensitive to psilocybin's effects, where a normal threshold dose of around 2 mg of psilocybin can result in effects usually associated with medium and high doses. Likewise, there are some people who require relatively high doses of psilocybin to gain low-dose effects. Individual brain chemistry and metabolism plays a large role in determining a person's response to psilocybin.

Psilocybin is metabolized mostly in the liver where it becomes psilocin. It is broken down by the enzyme monoamine oxidase. MAO inhibitors have been known to sustain the effects of psilocybin for longer periods of time; people who are taking an MAOI for medical conditioning or are seeking to potentiate the mushroom experience may experience highly potentiated effects.

Mental and physical tolerance to psilocybin builds and dissipates quickly. Taking psilocybin more than three or four times in a week (especially on consecutive days) can result in diminished effects. Tolerance dissipates after a few days, so frequent users often keep doses spaced five to seven days apart to avoid this effect.

Effects

The effects of psilocybin are highly variable, and dependent on the current mood and overall sense of well-being by the individual. Initially the subject may begin to feel somewhat disoriented, lethargic, and euphoric or sometimes depressed (depending on pre-existing mood (set)). At low doses, hallucinatory effects may occur, including enhancement of colors and the animation of geometric shaped. Closed-eye hallucination may occur, where the affected individual may see multi-colored geometric shapes and vivid imaginative sequences. At higher doses, hallucinatory effects increase and experiences tend to be less social and more introspective or entheogenic. Open-eye visuals are more common, and may be very detailed although rarely confused with reality.

Distortions in the experience of time in psilocybin-induced states have been subjectively reported, and objectively measured. In these studies, psilocybin significantly decreased subjects' reproduction of time intervals longer than 2.5s, impaired their ability to synchronize to inter-beat intervals longer than 2s, and reduced their preferred tapping rate. Recent studies into the effects of psilocybin on time interval reproduction may shed light on qualitative alterations of time experience in experimentally-induced altered states of consciousness, mystical states, or in psychopathology.

Users having a pleasant experience can feel ecstatic, a sense of connection to others, nature, the universe, and other feelings/emotions are often intensified. Difficult experiences or "bad trips" occur due to a variety of reasons. Tripping during an emotional/physical low, or in a non-supportive or inadequate environment (see: set and setting) could possibly cause anxiety or some sort of freak-out. Latent psychological issues may be triggered by the strong emotional components of the experience.

Some of these individuals report that they have experienced a "spiritual" episode. For example, in the Marsh Chapel Experiment, which was run by a graduate student at Harvard Divinity School under the direct supervision of Timothy Leary, almost all of the graduate degree divinity student volunteers who received psilocybin reported profound religious experiences.

In 2006, a group of researchers from Johns Hopkins school of Medicine led by Roland R Griffiths conducted an experiment assessing the degree of mystical experience and attitudinal effects of the psilocybin experience; this report was published in the journal "Psychopharmacology". Thirty-six volunteers without prior experience with hallucinogens were given 30mg. of psilocybin and methylphenidate (Ritalin) in separate sessions, the methylphenidate sessions serving as a control and psychoactive placebo; the tests were double-blind.

The degree of mystical experience was measured using a questionnaire on mystical experience developed by Ralph W Hood; 61% of subjects reported a "complete mystical experience" after their psilocybin session, while only 13% reported such an outcome after their experience with methylphenidate. Two months after taking psilocybin, 79% of the participants reported moderately to greatly increased life satisfaction and sense of well-being. About 36% of participants also had a strong to extreme "experience of fear" or dysphoria (i.e., a "bad trip") at some point during the psilocybin session (which was not reported by any subject during the methylphenidate session), with about one-third of these (13% of the total) reporting that this dysphoria dominated the entire session.

These negative effects were reported to be easily managed by the researchers and did not have a lasting negative effect on the subject's sense of well-being. Further measures at 14 months after the psilocybin experience confirmed that participants continued to attribute deep personal meaning to the experience. This research was widely covered in the major media outlets. The research team cautions that if hallucinogens are used in less well supervised settings, the possible fear or anxiety responses could lead to harmful behaviors (psychosis). Further studies by this group have investigated the relationship of psilocybin dose to likelihood of mystical experience in healthy volunteers and whether mystical experiences in volunteers given psilocybin can help with anxiety and poor mood due to cancer.

In rare cases, psilocybin use can cause Hallucinogen Persisting Perception Disorder. (Flashbacks due to "bad trips", auras and static around lights, depersonalization)

Social and legal aspects

Psilocybin and psilocin are listed as Schedule I drugs under the United Nations 1971 Convention on Psychotropic Substances. Schedule I drugs are illicit drugs that are claimed to have no known therapeutic benefit. Parties to the treaty are required to restrict use of the drug to medical and scientific research under strictly controlled conditions. Most national drug laws have been amended to reflect this convention, with possession and use of psilocybin and psilocin being under almost all circumstances, and often carrying severe legal penalties.

Possession and use of psilocybin mushrooms, including the bluing species of "Psilocybe", is therefore prohibited by extension. However, in many national, state, and provincial drug laws, there is a great deal of ambiguity about the legal status of psilocybin mushrooms and the spores of these mushrooms, as well as a strong element of selective enforcement in some places.

Because of the ease of cultivating psilocybin mushrooms or gathering wild species, purified psilocybin is often extremely difficult to find on the market.

Growing "Magic" Mushrooms (spiritual medicine)

Ok first off, I must say thanks to the innovators who have come before me, Psylocybe Fanaticus, Erowid and "The Magic Mushroom Growers Guide" (which is easily found on the internet), without their vast experimentation, and understandings I might have never "woken up" to the "True Reality" of things, grim as it may be. A very thorough step-by-step (although a bit scientifically expansive and therefore confusing and frustrating, due to different techniques) process can be found by looking up "The magic mushroom growers guide" on the internet. I'm the type of person who likes to simplify things so I'm just going to get to the point and detail the best way I've found to grow them (for educational purposes only, of course).

IT IS VERY IMPORTANT THAT YOU KNOW, CULTIVATION OF THESE "MIND EXPANDING" FRUITS HAS BEEN DEEMED ILLEGAL BY THE FEDERAL GOVERNMENT, AND PUNISHMENT CAN BE INCURRED FROM ANYONE BEING CAUGHT GROWING THESE "SHROOMS" FOR PURPOSES OF DISTRIBUTION.

The "psychedelic experience" is undoubtedly responsible for the entire "flower child", "hippie", 60's, 70's and "Woodstock" eras. Magic Mushrooms were at one time, sold legally in shops in Amsterdam all year long because they believed in individual discretion and freedom.

Another thing I must say is that the real "Magic" in these mushrooms, is their ability to separate your spiritual and physical selves, so that you can too have your own "religious experience". I cannot guarantee the safety of "wild" "magic" mushrooms, due to too many unknown variables (unknown toxins) in different contaminates (other types of fungus) that have access to the same growing media that the "shrooms" themselves come from. But undoubtedly, humans since the beginning of time have consumed nature's "Fruit of Knowledge" to find their spiritual selves. If you intend to look for natural "Shrooms", then consume them at your own risk. The hallucinogenic compound "psilocybin" occurs in over a hundred of different types of mushrooms and the only real "give away" to its presence in a natural "shroom" is, when you cut into, squeeze, or tear the mushroom, it should turn blue, which is a reaction to the psilocybin and oxygen.

The safest way that you too can have your own "religious experience", is by growing your own "Shrooms" on completely sterilized growth "cakes". When you manage to grow some of these "pure" (contaminate free) "shrooms", they are no more toxic than a cigarette, aspirin, or caffeine, and they definitely aren't poisonous. These "pure" mushrooms have the ability to help you on your road to enlightenment by helping you tap into the universal consciousness and the cash of information that is stored there. Buddhists call it gaining experience from past lives, Christians and Catholics call it invoking the "Holy Spirit", Indians and mystics call it a spirit journey. I call it an understanding of a truth that cannot be taught by another physical person.

The truth of the matter is that many people may not be able to go to a "level 5" "complete" experience. For a "physically bound" person it is a frightening experience. The purely physical mind and "ego" is not capable or comfortable accepting spiritual knowledge, and due to the separation anxiety that happens, when you become spiritually separate, your physical self "feels" as if it's dying, but it isn't actually "you", it is only your "ego" and your "physical nature" that is dying. But due to that "feeling" most people are simply too afraid to have a "full" experience.

These "Forbidden Fruit" have been used by Mystics, Indians, and Spiritualists, to gain perspective of themselves and the world, since before organized religion. True "mystics", "fast" for five days (don't eat anything, or very little and selectively for five days), before consuming their "shrooms", in order to purify their bodies, in order to have a more complete, spiritual experience. (They weaken their physical self, to empower their spiritual self.)

What you will need in order to grow "pure" shrooms (for educational purposes):

The "Shrooms" grow on sterilized vermiculite and brown rice flour "cakes".

So you will at the least need some medium grain vermiculite and some health food store "organic" quality brown rice flour. You will also need some distilled water (non-tap water is best) and some ½ pint mason jars. You must use ½ pint jars, 1 pint jars take too long to become ready and contamination usually results, ending in failure.

To get started, go to the local "Mart" store and buy some ½ pint mason jars, a Styrofoam cooler, some silicone, some cloth tape, some gallon self-lock bags, a box of 5 gallon extra large self-lock bags two foil deep baking pans, a foil cookie sheet, an ultrasonic humidifier, a metal grate (for the cooler), another metal grate (for the dehydrator) and an 8qt pressure cooker.

Go to the hardware store and buy a 5/8 drill bit, a piece of Plexiglas, some clear vinyl tubing, some grommets, some desiccant and some brackets big enough to fit around a two-liter bottle.

Most department stores do not carry vermiculite, only perlite, which won't work. To get vermiculite you need to go find a place that sells bulk lawn care and fertilizer items. That was the hardest thing for me to find but don't get discouraged, enlightenment is worth the work....

You will also need some "spore syringes". "Spores" are simply seeds of mushroom bearing fungus. These can be bought from any spore bank, there are many on the internet. Spores are completely legal to buy and ship as long as they are for "scientific studying purposes only". Simply look up the key word "spores". One of the best types for beginners are "Pesa" type, Psilocybe cubensis Amazon type, but my favorite is the "Orissa" type, for their incredibly large size capability and their original growing location was in Orissa India, along the "path" that Jesus supposedly traveled during his "missing" years from the bible. (The years between his youth and the age where his life became chronicled in the Bible, and other Gnostic, and Buddhist texts) He undoubtedly had access to these "mind expanding" fruits, and his belief in their abilities, might have been what caused the "Roman Catholics" (the same people who crucified him) to deem them "forbidden".

Spiritual origins of the Orissa strain:

A little bit more about the location in which the "Orissa" type shrooms were originally found, helps add to the understanding of their spirituality. They were found growing from a large pile of elephant dung (elephants are considered sacred in India), along the Narmada River at the foot of the Vindhya hills.

Narmada, a Sanskrit word means "One who endows with bliss". It flows from east to west and serves as the traditional boundary between North India and South India. (As we are in purgatory between heaven and hell) It originates from a small tank called Narmada Kund located on the Amarkantak hill.

Religious significance of the Narmada River: The Narmada happens to be one of the most sacred of the five holy rivers of India; the other four being Ganga, Yamuna, Godavari and Kaveri. It is believed that a dip in any of these five rivers washes ones sins away. According to a legend, the river Ganga is polluted by millions of people bathing in it. To cleanse herself, Ganga acquires the form of a black cow (an also sacred creature) and comes to the Narmada to bathe in its holy waters.

The place where it originates is named Amarkantak. It is a pilgrim town and a "nagar panchayat" in Anuppur District in the state of Madhya Pradesh, India. Also called "Teerthraj" (the king of pilgrimages), Amarkantak region is a unique natural heritage area and is the meeting point of the Vindhyas and the Satpuras (mountain ranges), with the Maikal Hills being the fulcrum. This is the place from where the Narmada River, the Sone River and Johila River emerge.

As the source of the Narmada, which is more than 150 million years older than the Ganga and is considered by many Hindus to be the most sacred of all the rivers of India, Amarkantak itself is sacred to the Hindus and is deemed to be a door-way to 'nirwana'. In the Amarkantak hills dwell some of the most primitive of the Madhya Pradesh tribals, the Hill Korwas and Pandavas. Even today, the Pandavas run away if they see any strangers approaching their village.

Religious importance of Amarkantak: Amarkantak situated on the western edge of ancient Kingdom of Kalinga is a place of worship for all the three worlds. Gods and Gandharvas (Celestial beings), Asuras (demons), Saints and Sages have all achieved great spiritual powers here. It is believed that whoever dies at Amarkantak is assured of a place in heaven.

Amarkantak is a Sanskrit word the literal meaning of which is immortal (amar) obstruction (kantak). The place was abode of Gods but was disturbed by the hindrances of Rudraganas and hence called Amarkantak.

In order to grow pure psilocybin mushrooms:

You need to combine measured amounts of the brown rice flour and vermiculite. I like to cook my flour and vermiculite separately in the oven before mixing to add to the sterility of the project. I put the bulk measurement of each ingredient into a deep foil pan and heat them both to 300 degrees in the oven for 30 minutes. I also add an extra quart of vermiculite to the pan so I will have enough for my dry layer. A barrier layer against contaminates.

The mix consists of 2/3 cup of vermiculite and ¼ cup brown rice flour for each ½ pint jar you intend to use. The typical 10cc spore syringe will prepare ten jars, so I like to prepare my mix in bulk. I mix 1qt and 2 2/3 cups of Vermiculite with 2 ½ cups of brown rice flour in a large mixing bowl which equals ten half pint jars. I mix the two in the bowl, with a butter knife, until I cannot see any separation of the different ingredients. That is the easy part. You need to boil the distilled water for about ten minutes to kill off any bacteria in the water. Once you begin to pour in the water, it will become much more difficult to mix, but you cannot stop.

The proper amount of water for each jar is ¼ cup of water for each ½ pint jar, but since I'm mixing in bulk, I use 2 ½ cups of boiled water for the entire amount in the bowl. Pour the water in a little at a time mixing thoroughly, difficult as it is (it almost feels like mixing concrete), until the mixture's consistency looks like oatmeal cookie dough with no obvious dry spots. (Yes, your arm will get tired!)

After you are done mixing, fill each jar with the mixture up to the bottom threads on the jar. Don't pack it tight, small gaps and holes in the mix are good! Wipe the tops of the jars from the bottom of the threads up, completely clean (spotless!) and then fill up (top off) the rest of the jar to the top with dry vermiculite. Make four holes in each lid before you put the lids on the jar. You make the holes for two things, first you need to be able to inject spores into the jar without opening the lid, and second, the jars will explode when you heat them up, if you don't.

After you are done filling, cleaning, topping off, and you've put your lid with holes in it tightly onto the jar, you need to cover the lids with tin foil so that when you boil the jars, water won't get into the holes and turn your hard work into mud.

Ok, the next step after you've prepared your jars is simple. The cheap way is to get a large pot and put as many of the jars in as you can. It's best to keep them off of the bottom somehow because the high heat will cause the jars to crack. I use a small metal grate, or a couple of wash clothes. Although cheaper, it's not as thorough. The best and fastest way is to use a pressure cooker. The jars need to boil in a regular pot for an hour which can dry out the jars. You don't want the jars floating; only put enough water in so that it comes up to a little past half way up the jars. With a regular pot, you need to constantly monitor the water level to make sure you don't boil away all of your water. It's cheaper, but it's a lot more time consuming and the margin for error and lost jars is greater. With a pressure cooker the time is cut down to about 25-30 minutes and your sterilization percentage is much better. Pressure cookers range from 35$ to 200$+, but the 35-45$ versions work great.

After you have finished cooking your jars, take them out of the pot and place them into self-locking bags and allow them to cool for at least six hours (overnight is best).

After the jars have cooled down to room temperature (between 70-82 degrees), it is time to inoculate (put the spores in). Shake your spore syringe well to make sure the spores are well dispersed into the liquid. You can insert the needles of your spore syringes into the holes you made on the lid. Make it so that the hole in the tip of the needle is facing the glass. Timing in this case is important. Most spore banks use dehydrated spores in their spore syringes. Once they prepare a syringe for you and ship it to you, it's only good for at most two weeks. It's best to have your jars prepared and ready to inoculate with spores on the day they arrive.

Now squirt just a little bit of the liquid into each hole in the lid. You only need 1 total cc. (a little extra won't hurt) for each jar, so the liquid should form a spot the size of a dime on the inside wall of the glass.

After you have squirted 1cc. into your jar put a piece of cloth tape (breathable) over each hole to prevent small bugs from getting in and messing it up. The cloth tape also helps protect against bad mold spores from getting in and contaminating your jar.

The next part is easy. Put them in a warm (80-82 degrees is perfect! Not over 85 or below 75), dark place and wait. (Don't get impatient, just let them do their thing) After a week you should begin to see small patches of white fuzz. That white fuzz is good, that's what you've worked so hard for. After two weeks you should be able to see large areas of the jar covered with the white fuzz. And after three weeks most of the jar should be white. Sometimes it takes longer but if your mix is right it should take no longer than 1 ½ months to become fully ready to "fruit". (If they aren't ready by then, something went wrong!)

After the entire surface is covered by white fuzz, inspect it very carefully to make sure there are no other colors. If there are other colors, throw it away! Other colors green, brown, pink, or anything except white, are signs of contamination and your media is bad. Don't risk it, just throw it away!

If the contents of your jar are completely white, (It can be beneficial to wait a couple of extra weeks after the jars are completely white to insure a massive initial flush of mushrooms, so don't rush it) then you are ready to birth your little beauties. But before you go popping the top on the jar, make sure you have a terrarium ready to provide your little babies a nice humid place to live.

This place is called a Terrarium. It is where your white cakes will live during the fruiting stage. It is inexpensive to build, all you need is a foam cooler with a tight fitting lid, usually 5-8$ at the local "mart", some silicone, and a clear piece of Plexiglas, 5-10$ at any hardware store. Perfect temperature and humidity can be attained by using an ultrasonic humidifier to force cool, humid air into the cooler; it frees up a lot of the work and keeps the environment in the cooler perfect temperature for the growth and fruiting stage. Ultrasonic humidifiers usually cost about 50$ but are well worth it.

Cut a hole in the lid of the cooler and silicone a piece of Plexiglas over it. Put a wire screen into the bottom of the cooler to keep your little white cubes off of the bottom. Make a small hole in the bottom of the cooler to let water and co2 (shrooms breathe oxygen and expel co2, like us!) out.

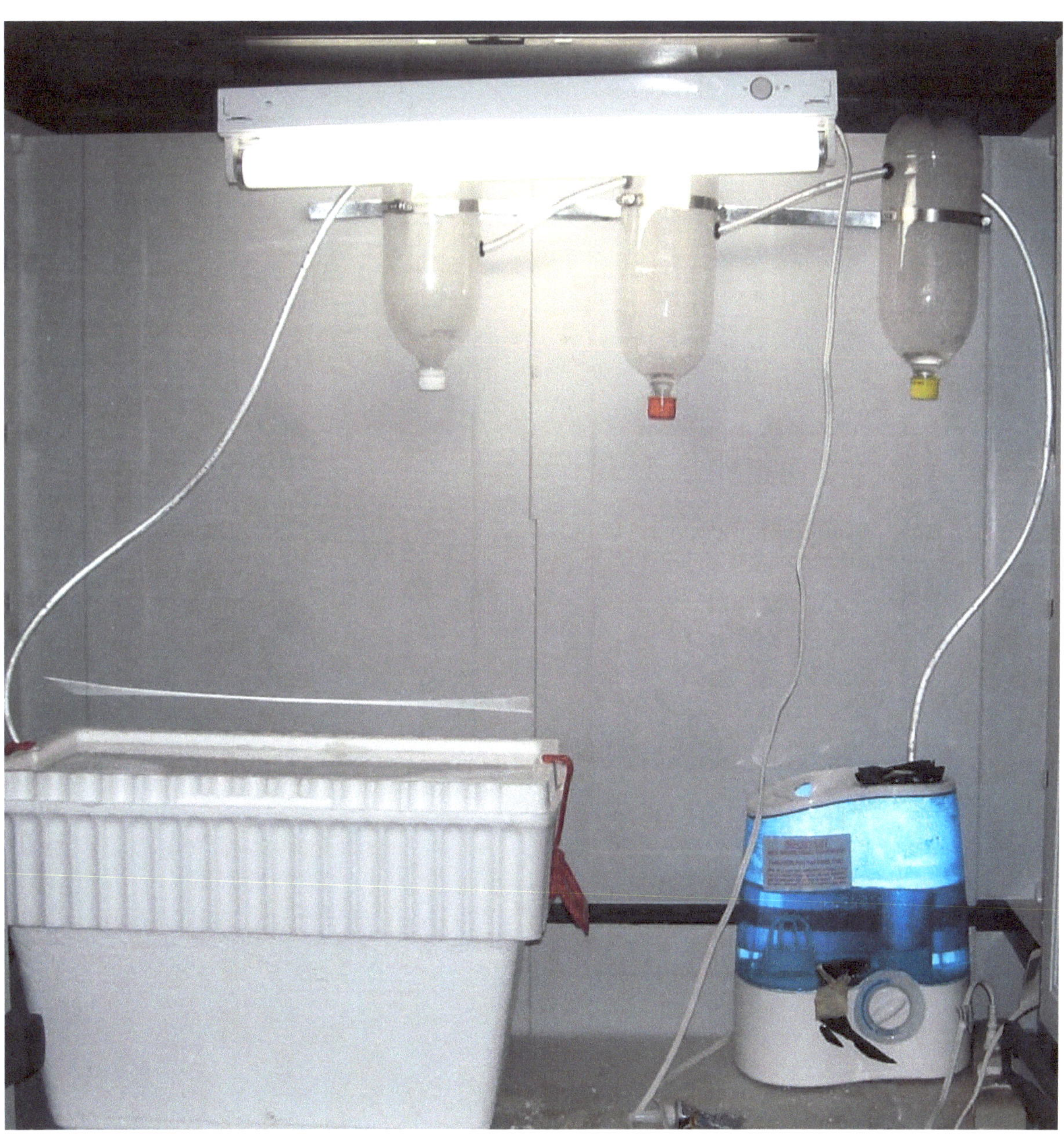

Ultra sonic humidifiers pump out too much humidity even at the lowest setting, so you need to build a drying chamber for the humid air. Don't worry, it's easy, three 2-liter bottles, some clear plastic tubing and some grommets and you have everything you need. I'm including a picture to show you the easiest proper design.

Face the top of the bottle downwards with the lid down, and drill a hole in the upper side, fit one of the grommets into the hole, then drill another hole into the opposite side farther down the side, and put a grommet in that hole. Follow the same process for the two other bottles and that part is done. I like to find a way to attach my bottles to a board. This can be done cheaply with tape, or you can get clamps at the hardware store.

Space the three bottles a couple of inches apart with the grommets all facing the same way, (high, low, high, low, high, low) and then cut pieces of tubing long enough to reach from one bottle to the next with a little extra length just for good measure. Cut the tubes at an angle so that a drop of water doesn't form and clog the end of the tube. It's also important that you don't have any low spots in your tubing, or they will plug up. Plug the regular opening that lets the humidity out of the humidifier and drill a hole into the center of the cap big enough to tightly fit the tubing into the top of the lid. Run a length of tubing from the humidifier into the first 2 liter bottle. Drill a hole into the side of the Styrofoam cooler towards the top edge. Run another length of tubing from the third bottle into the cooler and there you are.

I like to get a thermometer with a humidity gauge in it, to place inside the cooler so that I can tell at a glance, through the Plexiglas how the environment is doing without disturbing anything.

Once your Terrarium is up and running, you can go ahead and place your completely white little babies inside of the terrarium onto the grate. It is best if you barely handle them because everywhere you touch them, will not "fruit". I gently tap the jar onto its lid before opening the lid completely from the jar and then empty the contents into the lid. It should stay together (holding its shape) and slide out like a white moldy biscuit. Gently hold it in place as you flip it over and set it carefully right side up onto the grate. Remove the lid and let it settle into place. Put the lid with the Plexiglas back onto the cooler and bask in the glory of your accomplishment.

The white cubes need to be kept at mid to low 70's for a week or so at 90% humidity in order to start growing little shrooms. They need a little light, an arctic white or similar fluorescent bulb with a high blue content does well. I use a small individual light unit with my setup dedicated specifically for my "babies". I give my setup 12 hours of light a day, but they will grow with as little as 1-2 hours. I just turn on my light before I head out to work and turn it off before I go to bed.

After initiating these little shrooms, they grow to full size a little better at a higher temp, around 80 degrees. Seven to ten days after appearing, the shrooms will be ready to pluck.

After the shrooms grow to a larger size and begin to form the brown ball on the end, then the ball will turn into a cap. As the cap begins to tear away from the stalk it is time to pluck that shroom off of your cake. It is easiest to pluck the shrooms with a twist and pull method.

The best way to keep your shrooms edible is to dehydrate them. But you cannot use heat! The best thing to do is to get a cheap foil baking pan and put some desiccant into it. You can get desiccant at any hardware store by the name of "dampness remover", humidity remover, or something like that. It is usually in the paint section. Position a wire mesh over the foil baking pan and hold it in place with tape. Be careful to not allow the desiccant to touch the wire screen or your shrooms. Put the assembly inside of an extra large airtight locking bag, the 5 gallon type work well. After a couple of days they should be dry enough to save until you have enough for a complete dose.

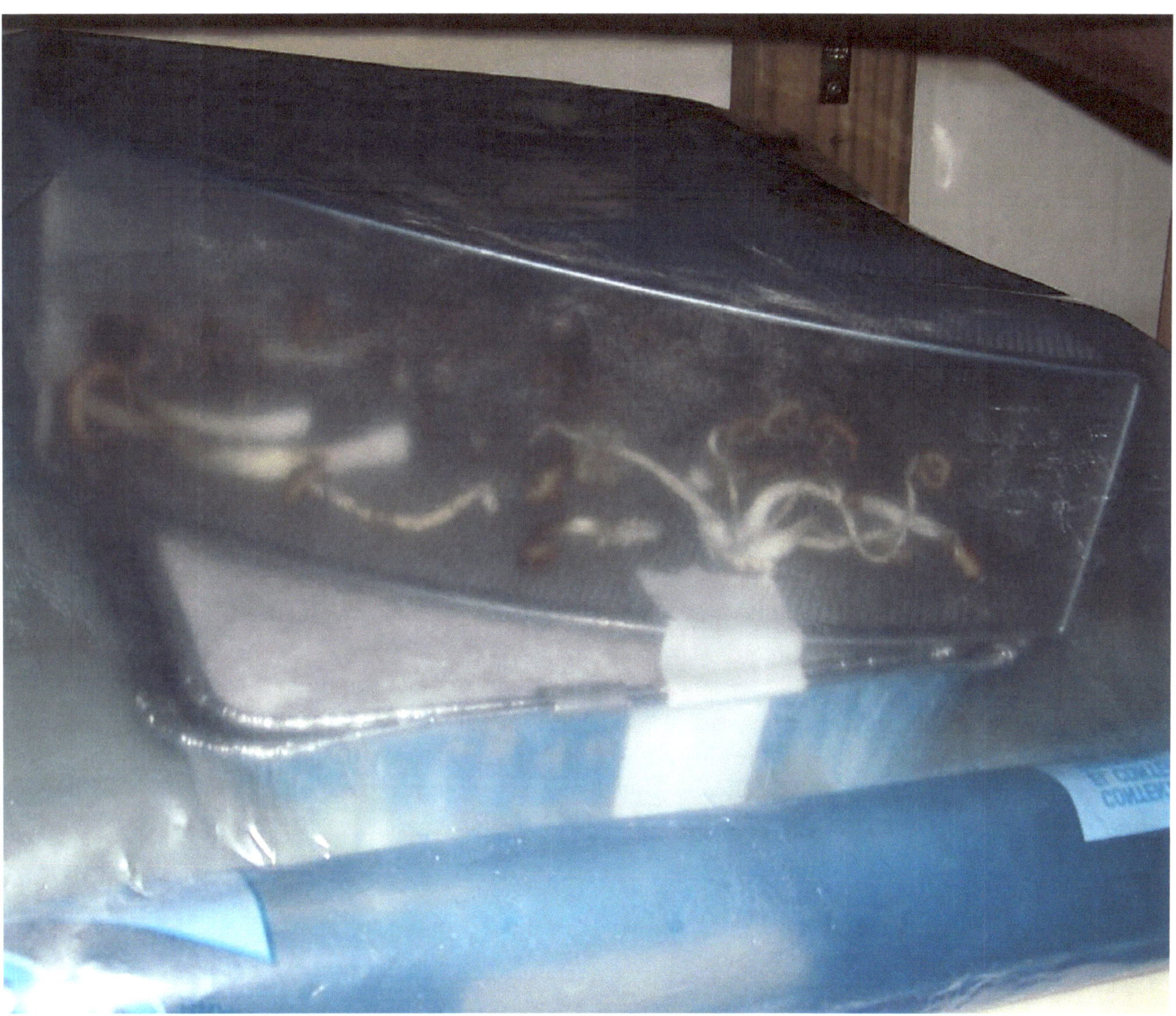

Dosage:

The typical amount of beginner "shroom" dosage ranges from 1.5 grams of dried shrooms for a mild experience, to 3.5 grams for an intense experience. My suggestion is to start with a small dose, until you get the hang of it, the feelings and thoughts that you will experience can be a little overwhelming if you don't know what to expect. You should under no circumstances eat more than 3.5 grams of dried shrooms at once if you are a beginner. Even experienced users have trouble maintaining their composure at levels above 3.5 grams. If what you are experiencing simply gets to be too much for you, then take a large dose 500-1000 milligrams of vitamin C, and that should neutralize the effect. But remember, once the feeling is gone, it's gone and eating more will not bring it back.

Do not eat shrooms more than once a month, not only does your body build up a tolerance to psilocybin, but you need to try and do something with the knowledge that you gained before trying to gain more. Take some time and reflect on your experience.

The most important thing is to remember: YOU ARE NOT DYING! Sometimes "ego" death happens, but that is not you! It is just your negativity! If you feel momentarily like you are going to disappear because you feel like you are leaving reality somehow, just try to calm your mind and pay attention to what you are seeing. What you are probably experiencing is a level 3-4 "trip". A trip of which allows you to experience a different "reality" (the spiritual reality). In order to experience the spiritual consciousness, you must leave the physical consciousness behind. Mystics and Native Americans used to go to that alternate reality all the time to receive help from their spiritual guides using peyote cactus or shrooms. But the truth is, you will not go, if you don't want to, it's entirely up to you. Remember, you are not going to go away and never come back, what you are experiencing is temporary!

Definitely, under no circumstances, should you go to the hospital. They will feed you some charcoal crap and cause you to have violent stomach cramps as they try to get you to throw up, which will do nothing for you. You will still be messed up and then also feel like crap with your stomach hurting. It will only cause them, to force you to talk to some psychiatrist who thinks they have the right to analyze you, when in actuality they need to pay more attention to themselves.

But ultimately you just need to let the psilocybin run its course. The hospital can do nothing for you. I started to freak out one time on some LSD (which is a hallucinogen, similar to psilocybin) and a good friend of mine said to me: "Don't worry bro, everything's ok, just ride it out" that seemed to make me feel better and the fear went away.

As far as the levels of psychedelic experience go, I feel like they are deeper levels of your own self that you are experiencing, or simply tests to be passed or failed. Failing these tests is common (and scary) for most and like any test, with practice, confidence is achieved and even the scariest barriers (like the fear of death) can be overcome.

Level 1-2 are attainable by most people and the good feelings are achieved by feeding your spiritual self.

Level 3 begins to become more intense, and your physical self begins to lose power as your spiritual self becomes more powerful. You begin to sense both of your "self's" inside of your body.

Level 4 Your physical self becomes weaker still, and begins to fall unconscious, when this happens, thoughts of death are common due to the physical self not wanting to relinquish control of your body. Your (negative) physical self uses that fear trigger to get you to maintain your physical consciousness, and therefore tries to prevent your spiritual self from taking over control of your body. If you have the presence of mind, it is possible to overcome that fear and take the final step to enlightenment.

Level 5 Your physical self becomes unconscious, although you are still alert and aware of your own consciousness, your spiritual self takes over and you become a completely spiritual being. Enlightenment is achieved and you become one with the universe, you understand transcendence and realize your own destiny. Congratulations, you passed your test....

In the end you return with the understanding that the only way in which that feeling can be made permanent is with the physical end.

The Gospel Of Thomas

The Gospel of Thomas gives insight into what Jesus was actually teaching his followers. It is through these sayings that we can see his mystical roots and his dedication to showing them the truth about the fruit of knowledge and that they needed to seek the truth for themselves instead of just believing what they were told by the Pharisees. Luckily it was preserved in the Nag Hammadi library, and saved from the destruction of the Catholic Church.

The Gospel of Thomas is a collection of sayings (parables) that the living Jesus spoke and Didymus Judas Thomas recorded. (See after for the Wikipedia definition)

1. And he said, "Whoever discovers the interpretation of these sayings will not taste death." *(The psychedelic experience, fruit of knowledge, teaches transcendence. Once you master transcendence, letting go of your physical self, you will realize that as your physical self dies, your spiritual self is simply waking up, and you are not actually dying. To fear death is to "taste" it, once you do not fear it, you won't taste it, and that's what the fruit of knowledge teaches us; not to fear death.)*

2. Jesus said, "Those who seek should not stop seeking until they find. When they find, they will be disturbed. When they are disturbed, they will marvel, and will reign over all. [And after they have reigned they will rest.]" *(This is a direct reference to the psychedelic experience. It encourages people to seek the truth, and not give up. Learning to give up your physical life is a disturbing feeling, but once you get past the fear, you will be amazed. Once you've conquered your fear of your physical death and can walk the physical world free from physical temptation, you will be superman {one who can walk the world without being affected by its negativity})*

3. Jesus said, "If your leaders say to you, 'Look, the (Father's) kingdom is in the sky,' then the birds of the sky will precede you. If they say to you, 'It is in the sea,' then the fish will precede you. Rather, the (Father's) kingdom is within you and it is outside you.

When you know yourselves, then you will be known, and you will understand that you are children of the living Father. But if you do not know yourselves, then you live in poverty, and you are the poverty." *(This refers to not believing what the "religious" leaders tell you to believe. instead one should look inside of their hearts to find the truth. During the psychedelic experience, many hours can be spent in deep introspective thought in order to find yourself.)*

4. Jesus said, "The person old in days won't hesitate to ask a little child seven days old about the place of life, and that person will live.

For many of the first will be last, and will become a single one."

(This statement refers to reincarnation and the spiritual knowledge of a child being greater than that of an adult who has locked away their spiritual knowledge to focus on physical knowledge)

5. Jesus said, "Know what is in front of your face, and what is hidden from you will be disclosed to you.

For there is nothing hidden that will not be revealed. [And there is nothing buried that will not be raised.]"

(Referring to HPPD, psychedelic (spiritual) knowledge that persists into regular (physical) reality. The physical world is an illusion or dream of our unconscious spiritual mind. Understanding this can unlock your understanding of the human condition)

6. His disciples asked him and said to him, "Do you want us to fast? How do you want us to pray? Should we give to charity? What diet should we observe?"

Jesus said, "Don't lie, and don't do what you hate, because all things are disclosed before heaven. After all, there is nothing hidden that will not be revealed, and there is nothing covered up that will remain undisclosed". *(This refers to the judgment and the understanding of the beginning and ending of time (time is a physical thing) the beginning of time is the beginning of your physical life. The ending of time is the ending of your physical life. Your entire life is the "life flashing before your eyes" moment, and we are all in our own judgments right now and we are being watched! Magic mushrooms show you that.)*

7. Jesus said, "Lucky is the lion that the human will eat, so that the lion becomes human. And foul is the human that the lion will eat, and the lion still will become human."

(This statement refers to reincarnation [rebirth] and the impurity of physical humans, which also becomes understood during the psychedelic experience)

8. And he said, "The person is like a wise fisherman who cast his net into the sea and drew it up from the sea full of little fish. Among them the wise fisherman discovered a fine large fish. He threw all the little fish back into the sea, and easily chose the large fish. Anyone here with two good ears had better listen!"

(This statement refers to becoming the "large fish" through spiritual growth so that you will be selected by God "the fisherman" when he seeks another prophet, as he chose Jesus. It can also relate to someone who has had a "level 5" psychedelic experience, and "comes back" as a prophet, with the goal of guiding others. The "large fish" is symbolic of someone who is receptive to spiritual guidance and willing to take a chance and believe the prophet, even though the prophet's teachings are different than what organized religions teach.)

9. Jesus said, "Look, the sower went out, took a handful (of seeds), and scattered (them). Some fell on the road, and they didn't take root in the soil and didn't produce heads of grain. Others fell on Thorns, and they choked the seeds and worms ate them. And others fell on good soil, and it produced a good crop: it yielded sixty per measure and one hundred twenty per measure".

(This refers to people who are suited to become disciples, the "seed" represents his teaching, (God's word) and where they fell, represented the people he taught, whether or not they accepted his teachings and spiritually grew from them. He of course is "the sower". The truth about the fruit of knowledge, "manna" is one of the seeds.)

I too have now scattered the seeds of truth upon you, will you allow them to take root in you? Or will you dismiss them and deny the truth?

10. Jesus said, "I have cast fire upon the world, and look, I'm guarding it until it blazes".

(This refers to his intention to spread the truth [as our physical prison which keeps us by our own choice] about the world of confusion which the Pharisees and the Catholic Church created by denying the truth about the fruit of knowledge, in order to undo it, and bring all of God's unconscious spirits back to consciousness)

11. Jesus said, "This heaven will pass away, and the one above it will pass away.

The dead are not alive, and the living will not die. During the days when you ate what is dead, you made it come alive. When you are in the light, what will you do? On the day when you were one, you became two. But when you become two, what will you do?"

(This refers to the idea of this world being similar to heaven, except as a negatively poisoned one which is quarantined distantly from the real heaven, with a spiritual unconscious "ward" where we are all "sleeping or unconscious", just outside of the gates to the real heaven. Once we are all cured of our unconscious states (our selfish physical poison), by eating "manna" then there will be no more "world", or the necessity for the "ward" in-between this world and heaven. It also references the light (the spirit world, see level 5 psych exp. and NDE), and how your one spiritual consciousness separated when it became unconscious and then that consciousness came into the physical world. It asks, "What will you do? Referring to the question, will you walk the physical path of death or the spiritual path of life?) You will begin to understand this at the "level 4" psychedelic experience.

12. The disciples said to Jesus, "We know that you are going to leave us. Who will be our leader?

Jesus said to them, "No matter where you are, you are to go to James the Just, for whose sake heaven and earth came into being".

(This refers to his teachings of the fruit of knowledge causing their spirits to grow enough so that they can look inside themselves for guidance. If they can go to James the Just, no matter where they are, then James the Just must be inside of them as a spirit guide. Referring to Transcendence/meditation)

13. Jesus said to his disciples, "Compare me to something and tell me what I am like".

Simon Peter said to him, "You are like a just messenger".

Matthew said to him, "You are like a wise philosopher".

Thomas said to him, "Teacher, my mouth is utterly unable to say what you are like."

Jesus said, "I am not your teacher. Because you have drunk, you have become intoxicated from the bubbling spring that I have tended."

And he took him and withdrew, and spoke three sayings to him. When Thomas came back to his friends they asked him, "What did Jesus say to you?"

Thomas said to them, "If I tell you one of the sayings he spoke to me, you will pick up rocks and stone me, and fire will come from the rocks and devour you.

(This refers to him wanting to know how his disciples saw him, he wanted to reinforce that he was not their teacher, he was just a guide helping them to see what was already around them the whole time, signs put there by the true teacher, God. The sayings he spoke were the Mystical/Gnostic secrets about this world being created as a trap, and death was the only permanent way out of it, but only once you are spiritually ready will you transcend back to permanent spiritual consciousness. He probably told Thomas about how he came to be as wise as he was, by eating the fruit of knowledge, and how others were not ready for that knowledge, and they would dispute the truth even if he told them)

14. Jesus said to them, "If you fast, you will bring sin upon yourselves, and if you pray, you will be condemned, and if you give to charity, you will harm your spirits.

When you go into any religion and walk about in the country side, when people take you in, eat what they serve you and heal the sick among them.

After all, what goes into your mouth will not defile you; rather, it's what comes out of your mouth that will defile you"

(This refers to putting too much emphasis on physical actions, which also becomes understood upon consuming psychedelic mushrooms. By fasting you will become hungry, and you are more likely to give in to temptation (physical desire) and eat impure things (as in meat). By giving to charity, you are simply spreading physical entanglements to others who have been gifted poor by God. Remember Jesus favored the poor. He felt that the poor (uncomfortable) were better suited to leave the "world" than the rich (comfortable). By praying for physical things you are walking the physical path. Heal the "sick" (the ones confused by the deceptions of the church) among them by teaching them the simple truth. By refusing food to someone who offers it to you, you might offend them and thus send them down the physical path of anger)

15. Jesus said, "When you see one who was not born of woman, fall on your faces and worship. That one is your Father."

(This refers to one outside of the physical world (a purely spiritual being), because to be in the physical world is to be born of woman. Yes, he was also born of woman! He was saying don't worship him!) The understanding of the difference between the spiritual world and the physical world is common after a level 4-5 psychedelic experience.

16. Jesus said, "Perhaps people think that I have come to cast peace upon the world. They do not know that I have come to cast conflicts upon the earth: fire, sword, war.

For there will be five in a house: there'll be three against two and two against three, father against son and son against father, and they will stand alone."

(This refers to the war in heaven in which this "world" was the result; it was his goal to help God undo this "world" by guiding us all out of our unconscious states, which is understood after eating the fruit of

knowledge, and having a psychedelic experience. His teachings were so powerful that one may become ostracized by his family after becoming spiritually conscious and then trying to guide others. It also refers to us all being "alone" in this world, regardless of "family", friends, or any other relationship attachments. One physical body cannot merge into another, and thus we are all spiritually alone inside of our physical bodies).

17. Jesus said, "I will give you what no eye has seen, what no ear has heard, what no hand has touched, what has not arisen in the human heart."

(This refers to spiritual truth, or God, because eye, ear, hand and even the human heart are all physical things, and spiritual truth, like God, is not physical. The psychedelic experience is not physical. It is spiritual. This is a blatant reference to the psychedelic experience.)

18. The disciples said to Jesus, "Tell us, how our end will come?"

Jesus said, "Have you found the beginning, then, that you are looking for the end? You see, the end will be where the beginning is.

Congratulations to the one who stands at the beginning: that one will know the end and will not taste death."

(Jesus' statement refers to a level 4-5 psychedelic experience, it also refers to coming back to spiritual consciousness, which is where we started and will ultimately end. Read the levels of psychedelic experience, specifically the part in the "level 5" that refers to the beginning and the end of time, and reliving their own birth. This is no coincidence!)

19. Jesus said, "Congratulations to the one who came into being before coming into being.

If you become my disciples and pay attention to my sayings, these stones will serve you.

There are five trees in Paradise for you; they do not change, summer or winter, and their leaves do not fall. Whoever knows them will not taste death."

(This refers to the spiritual awakening (coming into being, before permanent death) that happens after eating the fruit of knowledge. The part about the five trees is a blatant reference to the five levels of the psychedelic experience and also the mystical path. The part about the leaves not falling is a reference to a psychedelic mushroom being the tree of knowledge, and the person who knows this truth and uses it can awaken their eternal spirit and once that happens, you will no longer fear death, because you will know that death is not the end, you are just waking up.)

20. The disciples said to Jesus, "Tell us what Heaven's kingdom is like."

He said to them, "It's like a mustard seed, the smallest of all seeds, but when it falls on prepared soil, it produces a large plant and becomes a shelter for birds of the sky."

(This refers to heaven being spiritual truth and love for God, and once we are prepared to accept it, and consume the fruit of knowledge, then we will spiritually grow into a vessel for other spirits to work through.)

21. Mary said to Jesus, "What are your disciples like?"

He said, "They are like little children living in a field that is not theirs. When the owners of the field come, they will say, 'Give us back our field.' They take off their clothes in front of them in order to give it back to them, and they return their field to them.

(This is referring to the Gnostic secret of the world created by the Demiurge, and spiritual beings masquerading in this world to show other unconscious spirits the truth about the fruit of knowledge and guide them back to spiritual consciousness. Upon the "harvest" (rapture) these "undercover" spirits, will remove their physical forms and leave the negative physical world of the Demiurge.

For this reason I say, if the owners of a house know that a thief is coming, they will be on guard before the thief arrives and will not let the thief break into their house (their domain) and steal their possessions.

(This refers to the Demiurge and his minions trying to keep us imprisoned here in our spiritual unconscious state as their "possessions", as Adam and Eve were possessions of the Demiurge (Satan) Christ and his disciples being the "thieves" by trying to steal as many of the unconscious spirits as they could by teaching the

truth and leading them back to spiritual consciousness, by showing others the fruit of knowledge)

As for you, then, be on guard against the world. Prepare yourselves with great strength, so the robbers can't find a way to get to you, for the trouble you expect, will come."

(This refers to being spiritually strong, and understanding that the devil will use your physical desires to get to you. This is easily understood after a level 5 psychedelic experience.)

Let there be among you a person who understands.

When the crop ripened, he came quickly carrying a sickle and harvested it. Anyone here with two good ears had better listen!"

(This refers to "the rapture", in which fully grown spirits will be harvested from this "world", back to spiritual consciousness. Once you consume the "manna" your spirits will "ripen" (grow) and your perception will change to a spiritual consciousness, and then you will be ready to be harvested.)

22. Jesus saw some babies nursing. He said to his disciples, "These nursing babies are like those who enter the (Father's) kingdom."

They said to him, "Then shall we enter the (Father's) kingdom as babies?"

Jesus said to them, "When you make the two into one, and when you make the inner like the outer and the outer like the inner, and the upper like the lower, and when you make male and female into a single one, so that the male will not be male nor the female be female, when you make eyes in place of an eye, a hand in place of a hand, a foot in place of a foot, an image in place of an image, then you will enter [the kingdom]."

(This refers to the separation of the two consciousnesses, which you become aware of after consuming the fruit of knowledge and have a psychedelic experience, one being in heaven and one being here, once you become spiritually conscious here, you will realize we are all equal, the differences between male and female are only physical differences, in God's eyes there are no differences between either, angels after all are unisex! Once you become spiritually whole (alive), and surrender your physical self (ego) to God's will, then you will be eligible to enter heaven. At that point it will be like being spiritually born, as a spiritual baby)

23. Jesus said, "I shall choose you, one from a thousand and two from ten thousand, and they will stand as a single one."

(This refers to being chosen as "The Christ", the rare person who is willing to give up their physical life to become purely spiritual. This is the threshold you must pass to attain a "level 5" psychedelic experience. But once you have overcome the fear of "Death", you will not "taste" it.)

24. His disciples said, "Show us the place where you are, for we must seek it."

He said to them, "Anyone here with two ears had better listen! There is light within a person of light, and it shines on the whole world. If it does not shine, it is dark."

(Jesus used the fruit of knowledge to become spiritually awakened, and therefore discovered the "light" within himself. The light of God that shone through him upon the "World" by teaching all who would listen of God's intention for us all to use the fruit of knowledge to come back to spiritual consciousness)

(This refers to someone who has been "chosen" to become "the one", should they not use their gift of knowledge to save the world (by helping everyone understand) then they are basically denying helping God. Personally, I would never knowingly deny him!)

25. Jesus said, "Love your friends like you love your own soul, protect them like the pupil of your eye".

(This refers to trying to keep your friends on the spiritual path. Free them as you freed yourself. Prevent the negativity of the "world" from affecting them and pulling them down the physical path, through anger, lust, greed, etc.)

26. Jesus said, "You see the sliver in your friend's eye, but you don't see the timber in your own eye. When you take the timber out of your own eye, then you will see well enough to remove the sliver from your friend's eye."

(This refers to how it is easy to see what others are doing wrong, but one rarely thinks about what they are

doing wrong, once you master your own behavior, only then will you be ready to help your friend. A psychedelic experience is a deep introspective look at yourself and your own inequities. Only once you have completely surrendered your "self" to God, will you be able to convince your friends to do the same. In order to cure others of their negative selfish poison, you must first cure yourself. Surrendering your "self" to the effects of psilocybin, and having a "level 5" experience, is similar to surrendering yourself to Death, and transcendence. This is the lesson we must learn before we will be ready to transcend upon our physical death.)

27. "If you do not fast from the world, you will not find the (Father's) kingdom. If you do not observe the Sabbath as a Sabbath, you will not see the Father".

(This refers to denying (or limiting) worldly (physical) desires, in order to focus on the spiritual path which leads back to spiritual consciousness and heaven. This becomes understood upon a level 4-5 psychedelic experience. The Sabbath is meant as a day of worship and rest after consuming the "Manna", but I believe in worshiping every day (by focusing on how I can best help God reach the rest of his unconscious children), not just once a week)

28. Jesus said, "I took my stand in the midst of the world, and in flesh I appeared to them. I found them all drunk, and I did not find any of them thirsty. My soul ached for the children of humanity, because they are blind in their hearts and do not see, for they came into the world empty, and they also seek to depart from the world empty.

(This refers to how he became spiritually awake after eating the fruit of knowledge in "the world" and began to see how everyone is so full of teachings of people, who seek to mislead them, and about how they are unwilling to even consider that they have been deceived, he preached the truth and they refused to listen. He was sad for the children because they came into the world without any true spiritual knowledge, and because of their deceived parents not teaching them the true spiritual lessons that they need to know, simply because they don't know what to teach, their children will only be taught the physical path without ever striving for spiritual knowledge. We all need to eat the fruit of knowledge!)

29. Jesus said, "If the flesh came into being because of spirit, that is a marvel, but if spirit came into being because of the body, that is a marvel of marvels.

Yet I marvel at how this great wealth has come to dwell in this poverty."

(This refers to empowering your spiritual self by weakening your physical self. This is a blatant reference to the mystic practice of fasting before consuming the "manna". Also how great spiritual wealth (knowledge) can be found by even those of poverty. He himself was not financially wealthy but spiritually, he was wealthier than all. Spiritual wealth is priceless!)

30. Jesus said, "Where there are three deities, they are divine. Where there are two or one, I am with that one."

(This refers to being in the kingdom spiritually conscious after your physical death. The father (God), the son (the humble servant), and the holy spirit (the conscious spiritual relationship between the father and the son), he also refers to how his eternal spirit will try and guide all who truly seek the truth")

31. Jesus said, "No prophet is welcome on his own turf; doctors don't cure those who know them."

(This refers to how one who becomes "the Christ", a prophet, through dedication to an untaught lesson {fruit of knowledge}, will not be able to convince those he knew before his spiritual awakening, because they will not be able to see past his previous faults to fully trust in him.)

32. Jesus said, "A city built on a high hill and fortified cannot fall, nor can it be hidden".

(This refers to one who strives for (by consuming "Manna") and attains spiritual perfection (a level 5 experience), cannot be defeated, and through the work of teaching others will become well known).

33. Jesus said, "What you will hear in your ear, in the other ear, proclaim from your rooftops.

(He's referring to your spiritual ear, in which you receive spiritual guidance after being spiritually awakened by the fruit of knowledge, that's what you should tell others, not the deceptions heard by the physical ear)

After all, no one lights a lamp and puts it under a basket, nor does one put it in a hidden place. Rather, one puts it on a lamp stand so that all who come and go will see its light."

(This refers to what happens when one eats the "manna" and catches a glimpse of the spirit world and becomes spiritually awake, realizing the truth; they seek to tell all who will listen).

34. Jesus said, "If a blind person leads a blind person, both of them will fall into a hole."

(This refers to how confused unconscious spiritual priests in the luxurious church, guide other unconscious followers into confusion, possibly unknowingly, by denying the truth about the "Fruit of knowledge". They cannot teach the truth until they know it fully. The blind leading the blind, sadly that is the "world" as most know it.)

35. Jesus said, "One can't enter a strong person's house and take it by force without tying his hands. Then one can loot his house."

(This refers to how a prophet comes into "the world". By eating the "manna" one can become an awakened spirit undercover in physical form, who learns the ways of the physical world so he can effectively navigate his way through it to reach trapped unconscious spirits in order to free them" [loot the demiurge's house]) By exposing the temptations as they are, the spiritual one effectively prevents those temptations from having power (tying his hands).

36. Jesus said, "Do not fret, from morning to evening and from evening to morning, [about your food—what you're going to eat, or about your clothing-] what you are going to wear. [You're much better than the lilies, which neither card nor spin.

As for you, when you have no garment, what will you put on? Who might add to your stature? That very one will give you your garment.]"

(This refers to humility, eating and clothing are purely physical desires, a humble spirit thinks very little for food or clothing, he only eats what is required to remain in the physical world to further our spiritual Father's plan, not excessively, and only covers his physical form not to offend others, or inspire lust, not because they are ashamed).In your spiritual form, which you will become aware of during the level 5 psychedelic experience, you will no longer have the need for clothes, or the need to consume in order to live.

37. His disciples said, "When will you appear to us, and when will we see you?"

Jesus said, "When you strip without being ashamed, and you take your clothes and put them under your feet like little children and trample them, then [you] will see the son of the living one and you will not be afraid."

(This refers to the understanding that our "clothes" are our bodies for our soul, once we take off our physical form, identifying the physical form as death, and return to spiritual consciousness (life), we will no longer be afraid of death, because it was as simple as waking up. Only once we have attained permanent spiritual consciousness, after our physical death, will we see the son of the living one.) Magic mushrooms teach this very lesson.

38. Jesus said, "Often you have desired to hear these sayings that I am speaking to you, and you have no one else from whom to hear them. There will be days when you will seek me and you will not find me".

(This refers to how addictive the truth is. He was foretelling how the truth about what he was teaching (about the fruit of knowledge) would eventually be covered up by the church (by deeming them forbidden). He also foretold about how the church would tell lies "in Jesus' name" to lure people in, only to confuse them with more deception.)

39. Jesus said, "The Pharisees and the scholars have taken the keys of knowledge and have hidden them. They have not entered nor have they allowed those who want to enter to do so.

(This is a blatant referral to the cover up of the fruit of knowledge, by changing the name to "forbidden fruit", and changing the image to an apple instead of a magic mushroom, they effectively hid the keys to the gates of heaven, and spiritual consciousness)

As for you, be as sly as snakes and as simple as doves."

(Be sly by seeing through their deception (Use the keys of knowledge- "manna") and simplify your life by letting go of the physical and focusing on the spiritual, physical entanglements only complicate our lives).

40. Jesus said, "A grapevine has been planted apart from the Father. Since it is not strong, it will be pulled up by its root and will perish."

(This refers to this "World", it has been placed apart from the Father (outside of heaven), it is corrupted and once we have all returned to spiritual consciousness, God will end this world along with the corruptions in it)

41. Jesus said, "Whoever has something in hand will be given more, and whoever has nothing will be deprived of even the little they have."

(This refers to how ownership of physical things creates insatiable desire to own more things, whereas those who have nothing physical, will not be upset when nothing is deprived from them. The only thing they have is their physical life, if they willingly give that up, then they will be rewarded with spiritual life)

42. Jesus said, "Be passersby."

(This refers to what we all need to do in this temporal world. Come through this world temporarily without getting stuck on our journey back to spiritual consciousness [heaven])

43. His disciples said to him, "Who are you to say these things to us?"

"You don't understand who I am from what I say to you.

Rather, you have become like the Judeans, for they love the tree but hate its fruit, or they love the fruit but hate the tree."

(This refers to his disciples who knew him before he consumed the "manna" and became "the Christ", questioning and dismissing his teachings because they didn't believe he was a prophet of God, simply because they knew him as a physical person, a peer. They loved him as a friend but hated his new found spirituality because that way of thinking wasn't the way his friends thought. Or they loved his words but didn't want to lose their physical friend which they saw as inevitable)

44. Jesus said, "Whoever blasphemes against the Father will be forgiven, and whoever blasphemes against the son will be forgiven, but whoever blasphemes against the Holy Spirit will not be forgiven, either on earth or in heaven."

(This refers to never talking negatively about a relationship with God, to do so inspires others to do the same, which is doing the devils work) If you have the honor of receiving guidance from the spiritually conscious world in order to further God's plan, never ever talk poorly of that guidance.

I believe that I was guided to make these connections and put this truth out to the world.

45. Jesus said, "Grapes are not harvested from thorn trees, nor are figs gathered from thistles, for they yield no fruit. *(Physical people cannot produce spiritual gifts [knowledge])*

Good persons produce good from what they've stored up; bad persons produce evil from the wickedness they've stored up in their hearts, and say evil things. For from the overflow of the heart they produce evil."

(This refers to how a person's mindset is contagious. A good and happy person fosters happiness and trust in others, and an angry person fosters anger, hostility, and distrust in others, even if that's not what they desire.)

46. Jesus said, "From Adam to John the Baptist, among those born of women, no one is so much greater than John the Baptist that his eyes should not be averted.

But I have said that whoever among you becomes a child will recognize the (Father's) kingdom and will become greater than John."

(This refers to how we are all in this "world", born of woman; we should never take our eyes off of the spiritual path and become distracted by or attached to the physical world or anything in it. He also refers to the fact that we are all capable of becoming a conscious child of God, because we are already God's children simply unconscious. You will understand this if you have a level 3-5 psychedelic experience)

47. Jesus said, "A person cannot mount two horses or bend two bows.

(Referring to the two paths, or two consciousnesses, you must choose one. This is the lesson that magic mushrooms teach.)

And a slave cannot serve two masters, otherwise that slave will honor the one and offend the other.

(Referring to full commitment to one path, again you must choose, physical path, "sins"= demiurge (Satan)/ spiritual path, "virtues"= heaven (God))

Nobody drinks aged wine and immediately wants to drink young wine.

(Referring to how once you get a taste of the simpler spiritual path, after eating the "forbidden fruit" you will no longer desire the complicated physical path)

Young wine is not poured into old wineskins, or they might break, and aged wine is not poured into a new wineskin, or it might spoil.

(This refers to why a spirit is reborn into this world without any spiritual knowledge. You must forget everything (churches deceptions) in order to learn everything (spiritual truth). You can't teach an old dog, new tricks.)

An old patch is not sewn onto a new garment, since it would create a tear."

(This refers to the age of innocence, and how young children are not capable of learning true spirituality except by parable [fairytales]) One must experience the physical world in order to understand the lesson that physical desire only leads to unhappiness. Children are generally happy. Allow them to be that way through the age of innocence, so that they too can learn the lesson.)

48. Jesus said, "If two make peace with each other in a single house, they will say to the mountain, 'Move from here!' and it will move."

(This refers to one who unifies body and spirit, (By passing the test of the "level 5" psychedelic experience, overcoming death) and how every challenge they face after that will seem easy.) Once you face "death", the challenges of the physical world take on a whole different perspective.

49. Jesus said, "Congratulations to those who are alone and chosen, for you will find the kingdom. For you have come from it, and you will return there again."

(This refers to how we are all alone in this world, even if we have physical family and friends, we are still spiritually individual [alone], once you become spiritually awakened (by having a level 4-5 psychedelic experience) and accept spiritual guidance [chosen], you will understand the beginning and the end. You will understand that you are here for a purpose and understand what that purpose is (to guide others back to spiritual consciousness))

50. Jesus said, "If they say to you, 'where have you come from?' say to them, 'We have come from the light, from the place where the light came into being by itself, established [itself], and appeared in their image.'

If they say to you, 'Is it you?' say, 'We are its children, and we are the chosen of the living Father.'

If they ask you, 'What is the evidence of your Father in you?' say to them, 'It is motion and rest.'"

(This refers to our spiritual energy. Our spiritual selves are children of God, and our spiritual energy is what makes our bodies move. It is also our Father who will eventually call us home spiritually. [Physical death, a.k.a. "rest"]) By eating the fruit of knowledge and accepting what you learn from it, you will understand what it means to "come from the light".

51. His disciples said to him, "When will the rest for the dead take place, and when will the new world come?"

He said to them, "What you are looking forward to, has come, but you don't know it."

(This refers to the judgment, where you will be held accountable for everything from your entire life. Reviewing everything from physical birth till physical death, every second, that would be like living. We are all already dead (spiritually unconscious) and simply watching our lives play back in our judgment, without even realizing it.) Death is the loss of conscious thought. We all spiritually "died" when we were physically "born". In

actuality we simply fell unconscious due to a selfish poisoning, and we will only regain spiritual consciousness, once we use the spiritual cure, "manna".

52. His disciples said to him, "Twenty-four prophets have spoken in Israel, and they all spoke of you."

He said to them, "You have disregarded the living one who is in your presence, and have spoken of the dead."

(This refers to how his disciples mentioned other physical people (the spiritually dead) in "The world" who have spoken of the "messiah", instead of listening to his teachings. He had already used the keys of knowledge (psychedelic mushrooms) to attain spiritual consciousness.)

53. His disciples said to him, "Is circumcision useful or not?"

He said to them, "If it were useful, their father would produce children already circumcised from their mother. Rather, the true circumcision in spirit has become profitable in every respect."

(This refers to how we have all been made as we should be; we already have everything we truly need. Cutting back spiritual excess leads to spiritual simplicity.) Referencing the male penis in its uncircumcised form, it looks surprisingly similar to a beginning psilocybin mushroom. As the penis becomes erect, the head emerges, and the skin pulls and folds back resembling a maturing mushroom.

54. Jesus said, "Congratulations to the poor, for you belong to Heaven's kingdom."

(This refers to the sin of greed, and how monetary wealth is coveted by physical people. The more you suffer in this world, the easier it will be to leave it when the time comes, poor people aren't comfortable enough in this world to want to stay) When your "physical" life is over, will you be ready for it to end, or will you fight the end? You will understand this if you eat magic mushrooms.

55. Jesus said, "Whoever does not hate father and mother cannot be my disciple, and whoever does not hate brothers and sisters, and carry the cross as I do, will not be worthy of me."

(This refers to how one who is "chosen", must turn away from their temporary physical family, and also be willing to give up their temporary physical life in order to rejoin their eternal spiritual family) During the "test" which you take when you eat psilocybin mushrooms, you will be faced with the loss of everything you love in "the world", including your parents, children, friends, and even your own physical "life". Fear of loss will prevent you from passing your test, transcending and becoming one with the Holy Spirit (spiritually conscious).

56. Jesus said, "Whoever has come to know the world has discovered a carcass, and whoever has discovered a carcass, of that person the world is not worthy."

(This refers to someone who has had a level 5 psychedelic experience, which is like a near death experience, only temporary. This is what the fruit of knowledge does. It prepares you for the end of your physical life (transcendence). It shows you that you are already dead, and what you know as your "life" is in actuality your "judgment". The selfish physical people of "the world", are not worthy of one who stays in "the world" (the spiritually unconscious state), with full knowledge of their own unconscious spiritual condition. Whoever has come to understand this knows how to return to heaven (spiritual consciousness), but remains in the unconscious state in order to guide others, even though they may be ungrateful. "The world" is not worthy of one who is worthy of going to heaven, but stays in hell for the sake of others).

57. Jesus said, "The Father's kingdom is like a person who has [good] seed. His enemy came during the night and sowed weeds among the good seed. The person did not let the workers pull up the weeds, but said to them, 'No, otherwise you might go to pull up the weeds and pull up the wheat along with them.' For on the day of the harvest the weeds will be conspicuous, and will be pulled up and burned."

(This refers to the beginning of this world, how it was a nursery which was poisoned by selfishness and evil and how God told his angels not to remove anyone prematurely because they all have an equal chance to do good, through the use of free will. The "harvest" refers to the judgment in which our spirits are "harvested" from our bodies.) Once you have a "level 5" psychedelic experience and understand "the beginning and the end", you will understand this, for the psilocybin mushroom truly is "the fruit of knowledge".

58. Jesus said, "Congratulations to the person who has toiled and has found life."

(This saying refers to the test of the psychedelic experience and how you must overcome barriers within your own mind (toiled) in order to discover your true eternal spiritual self. How we can live an entire temporary physical life without ever realizing the temporal nature of that physical life, instead of realizing that we are eternal spirits which will exist after this temporary place (in everlasting life), and not to focus on the physical while forsaking the spiritual. One who has worked to see through the deceptions to find the spiritual truth.)

59. Jesus said, "Look to the living one as long as you live, otherwise you might die and then try to see the living one, and you will be unable to see."

(This refers to what the psychedelic experience does for you. It is spiritual training, it allows you to temporarily experience "death" (transcendence) in order to help you realize the spirit world is real, so that when permanent physical death takes you to the spirit world, you know what to expect and you become fully spiritually conscious. If you understand death as simply waking up, you will not fear it. By fearing passage to the spirit world, you effectively prevent yourself from going to heaven, simply because you don't understand it as it is, and it is in our nature to fear something we don't understand. That after all was one of the ways that Lucifer trapped us here in the first place, by making us fear our physical death. You can't see the top floor of the stairway to heaven from the first step.) He's telling us to use the "manna" to find our spiritual path, and then stay focused on that path in order to overcome this physical prison.

60. He saw a Samaritan carrying a lamb and going to Judea. He said to his disciples, "That person [carries] around the lamb." They said to him, "So that he may kill it and eat it." He said to them, "He will not eat it while it is alive, but only after he has killed it and it has become a carcass."

They said, "Otherwise he can't do it."

He said to them, "So also with you, seek for yourselves a place for rest, or you might become a carcass and be eaten."

(This refers to how this physical world and the Demiurge is consuming our spiritual energy in order to continue his spiritual life outside of heaven) Use the fruit of knowledge to understand that you are losing your spiritual life by staying in the physical "world", and "seeking a place to rest" means looking forward to a physical death in the name of God.

61. Jesus said, "Two will recline on a couch; one will die, one will live."

Salome said, "Who are you mister? You have climbed onto my couch and eaten from my table as if you are from someone."

Jesus said to her, "I am the one who comes from what is whole. I was granted from the things of my Father."

"I am your disciple."

"For this reason I say, if one is whole, one will be filled with light, but if one is divided, one will be filled with darkness."

(This refers again to the psychedelic experience. During a level 4-5 experience, spiritual/physical separation occurs, therefore physical movement becomes difficult (reclining on a couch), at that level, spiritual understanding occurs and physical desires are lessened or removed completely. Therefore your spiritual self will awaken and your physical self (ego) will die (only the states of mind live and die) (one will live and one will die). He also refers to how he fully went to the spirit world (a level 5 experience) back to full consciousness (whole) and returned to help others (was granted by consuming the fruit of knowledge- "the things of my Father"-God's mushroom).

62. Jesus said, "I disclose my mysteries to those [who are worthy] of [my] mysteries.

(This refers to why a physically dominated person has a hard time understanding the parables. His "mysteries" (teachings) are easy to understand for someone who has had a spiritual awakening (psychedelic experience). If you refuse to believe anything other than what the organized religions (Pharisees) teach, you will never find the "keys of knowledge" (manna) and understand the spiritual truth that he taught.

63. Jesus said, "There was a rich person who had a great deal of money. He said, 'I shall invest my money

so that I may sow, reap, plant, and fill my storehouses with produce, that I may lack nothing.' These were the things he was thinking in his heart, but that very night he died. Anyone here with two ears had better listen!"

(This refers to a physically consumed person. The rich person devoted his entire physical life to the physical path, never bothering to pay any mind to the spiritual path which he should have been focusing on. Everything in the physical world is temporary. Do not focus your mind on your temporary physical path. Use the fruit of knowledge to awaken your unconscious spirit. Once you've awakened your spirit, make your spiritual growth more important than your physical path so that when your physical end comes, your spirit lacks nothing (prepared for transcendence).)

64. Jesus said, "A person was receiving guests. When he had prepared the dinner, he sent his slave to invite the guests.

The slave went to the first and said to that one, 'My master invites you.' That one said, 'Some merchants owe me money; they are coming to me tonight. I have to go and give them instructions. Please excuse me from dinner.'

The slave went to another and said to that one, 'My master has invited you.' That one said to the slave, 'I have bought a house, and I have been called away for a day. I shall have no time.'

The slave went to another and said to that one, 'My master invites you.' That one said to the slave, 'My friend is to be married, and I am to arrange the banquet. I shall not be able to come. Please excuse me from dinner.'

The slave went to another and said to that one, 'My master invites you.' That one said to the slave, 'I have bought an estate, and I am going to collect the rent. I shall not be able to come. Please excuse me.'

The slave returned and said to his master, 'Those whom you invited to dinner have asked to be excused.' The master said to his slave, 'Go out on the streets and bring back whomever you find to have dinner.'

Buyers and merchants [will] not enter the places of my Father."

(This is a simple parable. It refers to how God has invited us all to return to spiritual consciousness (heaven), and due to most of us being consumed by physical desire (fear of death)(physically focused instead of spiritually focused) we choose not to go, even though we don't know what we're missing. Though those who are on the street (the poor), would be sure to come to dinner. The spiritually hungry would gladly take an offer of spiritual fulfillment.) Use the fruit of knowledge to understand the difference between the physical and spiritual paths.

65. He said, "A person owned a vineyard and rented it to some farmers, so they could work it and he could collect its crop from them. He sent his slave so the farmers would give him the vineyard's crop. They grabbed him, beat him, and almost killed him, and the slave returned and told his master. His master said, 'Perhaps he didn't know them.' He sent another slave, and the farmers beat that one as well. Then the master sent his son and said, 'Perhaps they'll show my son some respect.' Because the farmers knew that he was the heir to the vineyard, they grabbed him and killed him. Anyone here with two good ears had better listen!"

(This refers to how this world was once a spiritual nursery where spirits were grown and then harvested to be in God's kingdom, but the devil stole the nursery and it's crops from God (by hiding the truth about the fruit of knowledge), and everyone who has been sent to retrieve the crops (bring us back to spiritual consciousness by showing us the truth) has been hurt or killed (Jesus predicted his own death) by the demiurges minions (the church).)

66. Jesus said, "Show me the stone that the builders rejected: that is the keystone."

(This refers to how his teachings (The key to spiritual consciousness being psilocybin mushrooms) were rejected by the organized religions of the time, and how they deemed the fruit of knowledge "Forbidden")

67. Jesus said, "Those who know all, but are lacking in themselves, are utterly lacking."

(This refers to people who are wise only in the ways of the physical world, and know very little about their true spiritual nature. Psilocybin mushrooms allow you to learn about yourself through introspective meditation.)

68. Jesus said, "Congratulations to you when you are hated and persecuted; and no place will be found, wherever you have been persecuted."

(This refers to when you consume the fruit of knowledge and become spiritually enlightened. When you begin to guide others away from their organized religions who keep them confused, by helping them understand, those organized religions will hate you and will no longer welcome you, because you will be taking away their collections, and showing them as frauds, the same way Jesus did to the Pharisees and the Roman Catholic Church.)

69. Jesus said, "Congratulations to those who have been persecuted in their hearts: they are the ones who have truly come to know the Father.

(This refers to the inner turmoil that happens along the mystic path and when you've had a psychedelic experience. The separation of the spiritual self from the physical self and learning to let go of everyone you love in the physical world is the inner persecution that he's referring to)

Congratulations to those who go hungry, so the stomach of the one in want may be filled."

(This refers to the mystic practice of weakening the physical self by fasting before consuming the fruit of knowledge in order to achieve spiritual transcendence. Weakening the physical prison in order to gain spiritual fulfillment and freedom)

70. Jesus said, "If you bring forth what is within you, what you have will save you. If you do not have that within you, what you do not have within [will] kill you."

(This refers to faith and trust in God. While in the midst of a level 4-5 psychedelic experience, you temporarily experience physical/spiritual separation (an out of body experience), this is an experience that most of us sadly only experience upon physical death. The physical mind is incapable of comprehending the difference between temporary and permanent spiritual separation, so at this level a "bad trip" is commonly experienced due to the fear that accompanies that unknown experience. Although, if you have faith and trust in God, and believe completely that he only wants what is best for you, and surrender yourself completely to him, you will be "saved" on many levels.)

71. Jesus said, "I will destroy [this] house, and no one will be able to build it [...].

(This refers to the Gnostic belief that this world was created (or at least corrupted) by the Demiurge, and at this point it is considered a loss by our spiritual Father. He hasn't destroyed it yet due to the fact that the Devil still holds us hostage (in our spiritually unconscious state), inside of it and he loves us so greatly. Once we all use the fruit of knowledge to return to spiritual consciousness, the Demiurge will run out of food and his illusion will fail and he will die.)

72. A [person said] to him, "Tell my brothers to divide my father's possessions with me."

He said to the person, "Mister, who made me a divider?"

He turned to his disciples and said to them, "I'm not a divider, am I?"

(This refers to the difference between a physical father and our spiritual father. To care about a physical father's possessions is the physical (evil) path. Our spiritual Father's possession is simply love, and God's love cannot be divided. It can be obtained wholly simply by seeking it out and accepting it. Jesus did not deal God's love. He showed others how to find it for themselves, by giving them the fruit of knowledge and helping them have their own "level 5" psychedelic experience)

73. Jesus said, "The crop is huge but the workers are few, so beg the harvest boss to dispatch workers to the fields."

(This is referring to the need for more enlightened people to guide "the confused" back to spiritual consciousness. It also refers to Jesus' understanding that he could not complete his goal of awakening everyone in the world on his own, and asking for help from his apostles [more enlightened disciples]) He encouraged others to save themselves by using the keys of knowledge and then work to save others through an effort to spread the truth that the Pharisees and Catholic Church didn't want them to know.

74. He said, "Lord, there are many around the drinking trough, but there is nothing in the well."

(This simply refers to the total lack of spiritual truth in religion and "the world" in general. He was referring to the amount of people in the world who want to believe, but feel spiritually as if they are being mislead, because the church preaches deception (by deeming the fruit of knowledge "forbidden") instead of spiritual truth)

75. Jesus said, "There are many standing at the door, but those who are alone will enter the bridal suite."

(This refers to many people who seek spiritual enlightenment but don't know that they have two selves, the physical and spiritual. Once they use the fruit of knowledge to understand that and let go of the physical and become spiritually alone, can they attain spiritual oneness (the bridal suite) with God.)

76. Jesus said, "The Father's Kingdom is like a merchant who had a supply of merchandise and found a pearl. That merchant was prudent; he sold the merchandise and bought the single pearl for himself.

So also with you, seek his treasure that is unfailing, that is enduring, where no moth comes to eat and no worm destroys."

(This refers to the treasure of spiritual enlightenment (the knowledge learned by using the "fruit of knowledge" and having a "level 5" experience) which is permanent, and removal of temporary physical treasures, because nothing physical is permanent.)

77. Jesus said, "I am the light that is over all things. I am all; from me all came forth, and to me all attained.

Split a piece of wood; I am there.

Lift up the stone, and you will find me there."

(This refers to the feeling of oneness with the universe achieved with a level 4-5 psychedelic experience)

78. Jesus said, "Why have you come out to the countryside? To see a reed shaken by the wind? And to see a person dressed in soft clothes, [like your] rulers and your powerful ones? They are dressed in soft clothes, and they cannot understand truth."

(This refers to people who look to Jesus as a physical leader instead of seeing him as he truly was, a spiritual leader. It also refers to physical rulers and powerful (comfortable) physical people; not understanding spiritual truth because it is exactly opposite to physical belief. Spiritual truth will make a physical person uncomfortable. They do not try to understand spiritual truth because they do not wish to give up their comfort)

79. A woman in the crowd said to him, "Lucky are the womb that bore you and the breasts that fed you."

He said to [her], "Lucky are those who have heard the word of the Father and have truly kept it. For there will be days when you will say, 'Lucky are the womb that has not conceived and the breasts that have not given milk.'"

(This refers to the understanding that we are all born into hell (A spiritual unconscious state), and how our physical ties (children and family) keep us here, because one that has no children or family, has nothing to stay for, and in that respect, it will be easier for them to leave this physical consciousness behind and attain spiritual consciousness.) It is more difficult for one who has children to have the "level 5" psychedelic experience and master transcendence because the devil uses your love for them to prevent you from leaving your physical consciousness to achieve spiritual consciousness and oneness with God.

80. Jesus said, "Whoever has come to know the world has discovered the body, and whoever has discovered the body, of that one the world is not worthy."

(This refers to the understanding of the difference between the physical and spiritual selves. "Out-of-body" experiences are common when you eat psilocybin mushrooms and go above the "level 3" psychedelic experience. Once you understand "the world" as an illusion of your unconscious spiritual mind, and see your body as a mere suit, for your spiritual consciousness, the world of unconscious people will not be worthy of you, although that doesn't mean you don't still have a job to do. Wake everyone else up!)

81. Jesus said, "Let one who has become wealthy reign, and let one who has power renounce it".

(This refers to spiritual wealth (knowledge), and giving up control (power). What we need in this world is a

humble spiritual leader, capable of helping even the feeblest of minds, find their own spiritual truth, instead of some power hungry physical leader only concerned with their own superiority and controlling how others think and act (power).)

82. Jesus said, "Whoever is near me is near the fire, and whoever is far from me is far from the (Father's) Kingdom."

(This refers to spiritual consciousness. Through the 5 levels of psychedelic experience, one can come closer and closer to spiritual consciousness (transcendence), and with that knowledge, can begin to understand ascension to heaven (complete spiritual consciousness). "Near the fire" referring to the warmth of God's love, and "Far from the Kingdom", referring to how in an unconscious state, a person is far from consciousness, a.k.a. [dead to the world]). We are all distant from God, because to him, we are all unconscious. He created the "manna" to show us this very fact so we could wake up.

83. Jesus said, "Images are visible to people, but the light within them is hidden in the image of the Father's light. He will be disclosed, but his image is hidden by his light."

(This refers to the virtual reality of this world. As long as we are focused completely on our perceived physical environments, it will be difficult to see the spiritual path that had been right in front of us the entire time. We will only be able to see things completely clearly upon complete spiritual consciousness (physical death, either temporary or permanent.) At the "level 5" psychedelic experience, "physical reality" disappears, leaving only the spiritual reality. Once you experience it to that extent, you will look forward to your physical end, in order to remain spiritually conscious (with God).

84. Jesus said, "When you see your likeness, you are happy. But when you see your images that came into being before you and that neither die nor become visible, how much you will have to bear!"

(This is a blatant reference to a level 4-5 psychedelic experience. Ignorance is bliss. As long as you are only aware of your physical existence (The "self" you see in the mirror) you will not see anything wrong with it, and it is easy to enjoy. But once you have a level 4-5 experience and become "aware" of your "pre-mortal" existence, (spiritual self), and the evil, deceiving nature of your physical self, you will no longer be able to enjoy those physical activities as you once did. Once you truly learn your lesson, you cannot UN-learn it. It is a difficult task to explain this to a person who is physically consumed (spiritually unconscious) and has not eaten the "manna", but try you must!)

85. Jesus said, "Adam came from great power and great wealth, but he was not worthy of you. For had he been worthy, [he would] not [have tasted] death."

(This refers to Adam only eating of the "forbidden fruit" once, and after that deciding not to eat it again out of fear of death, and therefore choosing not to return to full spiritual consciousness. Instead he chose to further follow his physical path, by pursuing Eve, and fathering physical children.)

86. Jesus said, "[Foxes have] their dens and birds have their nests, but human beings have no place to lay down and rest."

(This refers to the understanding that we as humans (our spiritual selves) were never meant for this (physical) world. Every creature in this world has a purpose. They all have a part to play in the bigger picture, except us. Physical humans are consumers. We are consuming this planet instead of protecting it, just like the Demiurge consumes us. We are meant to use the manna and transcend to spiritual consciousness. We have overstayed our time here.)

87. Jesus said, "How miserable is the body that depends on a body, and how miserable is the soul that depends on these two."

(This refers to being in this world as a spiritual person after using the keys of knowledge (manna), with the understanding that in order to fulfill your purpose in this world (spiritually awakening others) you have to continue operating your physical body (vessel), even though you would rather not because you understand its evil nature and see it as a channel for evil through its own insatiable physical desires. Physically consumed people are also miserable even though they don't know it, again ignorance is bliss)

88. Jesus said, "The messengers and the prophets will come to you and give you what belongs to you. You, in turn, give them what you have, and say to yourselves, 'When will they come and take what belongs to them?"

(This refers to spiritual consciousness. The true messengers and prophets will give you spiritual truth (forbidden fruit) and help guide you back to spiritual consciousness, therefore giving you your true self and your own salvation. In turn you should give them your unnecessary physical possessions to help further their work (helping others). Once you become spiritually "awake", you will long for God's angels to come back and reclaim you, for it is your spiritual self who belongs to God and his angels (his angels being an extension of him and his kingdom) The Holy Spirit)

89. Jesus said, "Why do you wash the outside of the cup? Don't you understand that the one who made the inside is also the one who made the outside?

(This refers to spiritual cleansing. Many people focus on cleaning their physical selves (bodies), but their spiritual selves are filthy. Instead we should focus less on our physical selves and concentrate more on our spiritual selves.) Eat the "manna" and you will understand.

90. Jesus said, "Come to me, for my yoke is comfortable and my lordship is gentle, and you will find rest for yourselves."

(This refers to spiritual consciousness, "rest" meaning physical death. When you separate from your physical self, your spiritual self is released from the work of making your physical self function. Released from work= rest) The will of God (to awaken his spiritual children) is a spiritually rewarding job and is not difficult for one with the Holy Spirit.

91. They said to him, "Tell us who you are so that we may believe in you."

He said to them, "You examine the face of heaven and earth, but you have not come to know the one who is in your presence, and you do not know how to examine the present moment."

(This refers to their spiritually unconscious selves, that God is with them spiritually they just don't know it because they are spiritually unconscious. They don't realize the present moment is a moment of eternity (our entire physical lives go by in a mere moment of eternity) in which we are all judged (also known as life, yes, this is that moment). Eat the "manna" and you will understand.

92. Jesus said, "Seek and you will find".

In the past however, I did not tell you the things about which you asked me then. Now I am willing to tell them, but you are not seeking them."

(This refers to his physically concerned disciples, asking him to give them pure, spiritual truths, but due to their focus on their physical path, those truths were withheld from them because Jesus knew they wouldn't understand, and because they couldn't fully deny their physical path, they are still not seeking his spiritual wisdom.) Seek the truth about the "forbidden fruit" for yourself and you will find it.

93. Don't give what is holy to dogs, for they might throw them upon the manure pile. Don't throw pearls [to] pigs, or they might [defile]... it [...]."

(This refers to his teachings about the "keys of knowledge" and the documentations of his sermons. His references to dogs and pigs, were meant to represent the luxurious Roman Catholic Church, and other powerful organized religions who sought to undo his teaching of the "forbidden" fruit of knowledge and deem it "heretical")

94. Jesus [said], "One who seeks will find, and for [one who knocks] it will be opened."

(This refers to a person who takes it upon themselves to find God and his Kingdom (salvation), instead of relying on organized religion to "save" them; you "seek" when you eat psilocybin mushrooms and have a level 5 psychedelic experience.)

95. [Jesus said], "If you have money, don't lend it at interest. Rather, give [it] to someone from whom you won't get it back."

(This simply refers to not caring for physical wealth as much as the spiritual happiness of helping others. Do not value physical things. Value spiritual knowledge above all and give that to everyone you can)

96. Jesus [said], "The Father's kingdom is like [a] woman. She took a little heaven, [hid] it in dough, and made it into large loaves of bread. Anyone here with two ears had better listen!"

(This refers to how this world was designed as a spiritual nursery in which to grow spirits for our spiritual Father's kingdom. A little bit of spiritual energy grows in each of us until it is ready to be removed. It could also be a reference to baking with "manna".)

97. Jesus said, "The [Father's] kingdom is like a woman who was carrying a [jar] full of meal. While she was walking along [a] distant road, the handle of the jar broke and the meal spilled behind her along the road. She didn't know it; she hadn't noticed a problem. When she reached her house, she put the jar down and discovered that it was empty."

(This refers to how things are. We do not know that there is a problem until it is too late. In other words, we go through our entire physical lives on the road of life, being drained of our spiritual energy, without knowing it, until we reach the end, only to realize that we no longer have any left and realize it's too late to get any of it back) By using the "manna" as a way to stop the spiritual drainage, you can stop "the problem".

98. Jesus said, "The Father's Kingdom is like a person who wanted to kill someone powerful. While still at home he drew his sword and thrust it into the wall to find out whether his hand would go in. Then he killed the powerful one."

(This refers to devaluing physical things in order to kill your insatiable physical desires, (the powerful one)) Once you use the "manna", your spiritual self will wake up and you will understand physical things don't matter, and the physical temptations will lose their power over you.

99. The disciples said to him, "Your brothers and your mother are standing outside."

He said to them, "Those here who do what my Father wants are my brothers and my mother. They are the ones who will enter my Father's kingdom."

(This refers to his and the Apostles mission of trying to guide others back to spiritual consciousness, (by teaching about the "keys of knowledge" because that is God's plan, to wake up all of his unconscious spiritual children. He was referring to spiritual family which can be different than physical family).

100. They showed Jesus a gold coin and said to him, "The Roman emperor's people demand taxes from us."

He said to them, "Give the emperor what belongs to the emperor, give God what belongs to God, and give me what is mine."

(This refers to how government (the devil's minions) made the money in order to enslave people. It came from them and therefore it belongs to them, they just loan it to us (at interest, "taxes"). God gave us our soul, (spiritual energy) it came from him and therefore it belongs to him. Jesus gave spiritual truth, and all he wants is to help God by guiding others back to spiritual consciousness, completing his duty. To believe in his teachings (of the fruit of knowledge) and understand them and therefore returning to spiritual consciousness, through trust in God through him, gives him honor. Jesus only wanted the satisfaction of successfully completing the task that god put before him, which was to guide all the people of the world back to spiritual consciousness.) Don't work for money. Work to complete God's will.

101. "Whoever does not hate [father] and mother as I do cannot be my [disciple], and whoever does [not] love [father and] mother as I do cannot be my [disciple]. For my mother [...], but my true [mother] gave me life."

(This refers to knowing the difference between physical father and mother, and spiritual Father and Mother. To understand that our physical parents unknowingly imprisoned us spiritually in our physical forms an imperfect world run by the Demiurge will cause us to see them negatively [hate]. In turn, God is both our Spiritual Father and Mother in one, and it is from God that we have our spiritual energy and life; therefore we should love God with all our soul as Jesus did. Ultimate devotion to God our spiritual father is being willing to

give up your physical life to return to him, as Jesus did!)

102. Jesus said, "Damn the Pharisees! They are like a dog sleeping in the cattle manger: the dog neither eats nor [lets] the cattle eat."

(This refers to how "organized" religious leaders don't follow their true spiritual path (by denying the truth about the "fruit of knowledge", and in turn force the confused followers of "their" religions to follow the physical path even though they desire to follow their spiritual path. Because they do not strive for spiritual perfection, they do not allow or help others attain spiritual perfection) Instead of teaching people how to live "properly" religion should show people how to die "properly". This is the "knowledge" learned from the "fruit of knowledge".

103. Jesus said, "Congratulations to those who know where the rebels are going to attack. [They] can get going, collect their imperial resources, and be prepared before the rebels arrive."

(This refers to the war in heaven and Armageddon and "the rapture". To understand that this world is the battle ground where the battle is fought inside each and every one of us, [the battle between our physical and spiritual sides] enables us to win our own personal battles and be able to overcome any negative attack on our positive spirits. Luck favors the prepared.)

104. They said to Jesus, "Come, let us pray today, and let us fast."

Jesus said, "What sin have I committed, or how have I been undone? Rather, when the groom leaves the bridal suite, then let people fast and pray."

(This refers to the intimate relationship between one who is totally committed to God and God. He has no need to specifically pray, because his mind is constantly praying already [internally walking the spiritual path]. When a person gives into physical desire [sins] and forsakes their spiritual path [intimate relationship with God] only then do they need to refocus themselves on their spiritual path through prayer and physical self denial [fasting])

105. Jesus said, "Whoever knows the father and the mother will be called the child of a whore".

(This reference relates to the ancient view of heresy. Due to Jesus' proclamation that he was a child of God, or a son of God, he was deemed a heretic.) A "heretic" being viewed negatively like a physical fatherless child of a whore.

106. Jesus said, "When you make the two into one, you will become children of Adam, and when you say, 'Mountain, move from here!' it will move."

(This refers to the spiritual awakening that happens upon a conscious level 5 psychedelic experience. Once you become fully spiritually conscious (and one with God), no physical barrier will be able to stand before you. There will be no challenge in the physical world too difficult for you to overcome)

107. Jesus said, "The (Father's) Kingdom is like a shepherd who had a hundred sheep. One of them, the largest, went astray. He left the ninety-nine and looked for the one until he found it. After he had toiled, he said to the sheep, 'I love you more than the ninety-nine.'"

(This refers to us. We (our spiritual selves) are God's sheep and he is our shepherd. The more committed we are to our spiritual path the larger our spiritual selves grow. Once we've committed ourselves fully to our spiritual path, our shepherd will work to keep us on that path instead of going astray down the physical path.) Full commitment is what's required to attain the "level 5" psychedelic experience. Fear is the absence of love.

108. Jesus said, "Whoever drinks from my mouth will become like me; I myself shall become that person, and the hidden things will be revealed to him."

(This refers to his teachings (of the keys of knowledge, "manna"). To accept his teaching and understand it (as unorthodox and different as it was), is symbolized by "drinking from his mouth". It refers to anyone having the ability to become "the Christ", by using the "fruit of knowledge" to come to understand "the world" as it truly is (the hidden truth will be revealed).)

109. Jesus said, "The (Father's) kingdom is like a person who had a treasure hidden in his field but did not know it. And [when] he died he left it to his [son]. The son [did] not know about it either. He took over the

field and sold it. The buyer went plowing, [discovered] the treasure, and began to lend money at interest to whomever he wished."

(This refers to the understanding that our spiritual guidance (cure) grows naturally all over the world (our field), but due to it being deemed "forbidden", and its image changed to an apple, it has been hidden from us. Centuries have gone by and generations have come and gone from the "field", but the spiritual truth is trying to come out and I (the buyer) have figured it out and wish to pass it to you)

110. Jesus said, "Let one who has found the world, and has become wealthy, renounce the world."

(This refers to someone who has had a level 3-4 psychedelic experience, and has become spiritually wealthy. At this level most people are gripped by fear of leaving "the world", because what lies beyond is difficult to understand, and we always fear what we don't understand. In order to become spiritually conscious, (a "level 5" experience) one needs to surrender completely, and let go (renounce) of everything in "the world". Even temporarily)

111. Jesus said, "The heavens and the earth will roll up in your presence, and whoever is living from the living one will not see death."

(This refers to a level 5 psychedelic experience, in which a complete separation from this physical reality is experienced and one becomes in unity with God, although even a level 5 experience is temporary, the spiritual knowledge you gain cannot be dismissed, and the fear of permanent physical death disappears (therefore you will not see or taste it), because you are not "dying", you are just waking up)

Does not Jesus say, "Those who have found themselves, of them the world is not worthy"?

112. Jesus said, "Damn the flesh that depends on the soul. Damn the soul that depends on the flesh."

(This refers to our evil physical bodies with all of their insatiable desires and how our spirits provide the energy for them to work. The flesh is evil and in turn the soul that gives in (surrenders control, becomes a slave) to the flesh's evil insatiable physical desires (the pleasures of the flesh) is damned to suffer its fate (death)). By eating the "manna" (psilocybin mushrooms) you are seeking to learn how to let go of the flesh.

113. His disciples said to him, "When will the kingdom come?"

"It will not come by watching for it. It will not be said, 'Look here!' or 'Look, there!' Rather, the Father's kingdom is spread out upon the earth, and people don't see it."

(This refers to magic mushrooms, and how they grow all over the earth, and due to the fact that the church has hidden the truth about them by changing the name and the image, and deeming them forbidden, people don't see them as they are". We must all seek it out to learn it (experience it) for ourselves, no one can take you to (or show you) the kingdom (spiritual consciousness). Eat magic mushrooms and have a "level 5" psychedelic experience to understand.

114. Simon Peter said to them, "Make Mary leave us, for females don't deserve life".

Jesus said, "Look, I will guide her to make her male, so that she too may become a living spirit resembling you males. For every female who makes herself male will enter the kingdom of Heaven".

(This refers to the idea that physical women are evil because they seek the attention of males and by drawing the attention of males, they draw males down a physical path. Women were created to be attractive to males so that physical offspring could be produced in order to further the demiurges plan. Women seek to control the thoughts of men. Those women, who overcome their desire for attention and put on the mindset of a spiritual guide instead of a physical distraction, can also attain spiritual perfection.)

Everyone regardless of the differences between male and female are capable of overcoming their physical natures. This is easily understood after eating magic mushrooms.

This is an excerpt from the Wikipedia reference on the Gospel of Thomas

The Gospel according to Thomas, also known as The Gospel of Thomas, is a New Testament-era apocryphon, nearly completely preserved in a Coptic papyrus manuscript discovered in 1945 at Nag Hammadi,

Egypt.

The text is in the form of a codex, bound in a method now called Coptic binding. It was written for a school of early Christians who claimed Thomas the Apostle as their founder. *Unlike the four canonical gospels, The Gospel of Thomas is not a narrative account of the life of Jesus, and is not worked into any overt philosophical or rhetorical context. Rather, it is "Logia", or gospel sayings, with short dialogues and sayings attributed to Jesus. (His simply mystic parable teachings)*

In the "incipit", the writer is styled Didymus Judas Thomas. "Didymus" (Greek) and "Thomas" (Hebrew) both mean "twin", and the name "Judas", also Jude or Judah, is the angelicized Greek rendering of the Hebrew name "Yehudah".

The work comprises 114 sayings attributed to Jesus. Some of these sayings resemble those found in the four canonical Gospels (Matthew, Mark, Luke, and John), while others were not known until its discovery. No major Christian group accepts this gospel as canonical or authoritative.

When the Coptic version of the complete text of "Thomas" was found, scholars realized that three separate portions of a Greek version of it had already been discovered in Oxyrhynchus, seemingly originating from the same collection of sayings bearing the Greek fragments of the "Gospel of Thomas" dating from between AD 200 to AD250, with another Greek fragment discovered in 1905 predating AD200; the manuscript of the Coptic version dates to about 340. Although the Coptic version is not quite identical to any of the Greek fragments, it is believed that the Coptic version was translated from an earlier Greek version, itself recorded from an earlier oral version.

The original text was published in photographic facsimile in 1975. The James M. Robinson translation was first published in 1977, as part of "The Nag Hammadi Library in English". The Gospel of Thomas has been translated and annotated in several languages. The original manuscript is the property of Egypt's Department of Antiquities. The first photographic edition was published in 1956, and its first critical analysis appeared in 1959.

The Gospel of Thomas and The canon of the New Testament

The New Testament was becoming more accepted by 140, but it had also become widely accepted that other texts formed parts of the records of the life and ministry of Jesus. Although arguments about some potential New Testament books, such as the "Shepherd of Hermas" and "The Book of Revelation", continued well into the 4th century, four canonical gospels, attributed to Matthew, Mark, Luke, and John, were accepted among orthodox Christians at least as early as the mid-2nd century. Tatian's widely used "Diatessaron", compiled between 160 and 175, utilized the four gospels without any consideration of others.

It should be noted that information about the historical Jesus itself was not a singular criterion for inclusion into the New Testament Canon. Not all of the books that ended up in the New Testament contain information about the historical Jesus, nor teachings from the historical Jesus, such as the Epistles and the book of Revelation.

The "Gospel of Thomas" may have been excluded from the canon of the New Testament because it was believed:

Reasoning of Roman Catholics

1. Not to have been written close to the time of Jesus
2. Not to have been written by apostolic authority or was forged in Thomas' name
3. Not to have been used by multiple churches over a wide geographic range
4. To be heretical or unorthodox

(This just goes to show that the Roman Catholic Church is simply trying to keep us in the dark. Why would they not encourage us to learn all we can, and decide for ourselves what is right?)

The reasoning I believe they have kept Jesus' true teachings secret:

1. *The true teachings of Jesus stood to simplify peoples understanding of God and Heaven.*

2. If everyone realized they didn't need to go to "church" to worship, it would mean the end of the Catholic Church's power and wealth.

3. Jesus' true message was designed exactly opposite of what the church was teaching and therefore even Jesus was deemed a "Heretic" (by them!).

The Theology of the Gospel of Thomas

The Gospel of Thomas begins, "These are the secret sayings that the living Jesus spoke and which Didymos Judas Thomas recorded." Both the words "Didymos" (Greek) and "Thomas" (Hebrew) mean "Twin" and are not actually names. Rather the author's surname is Judas or Jude, who is – according to Catholic Church tradition – The Apostle Jude who is credited as having penned the canonical Epistle of Jude and is also called the Apostle Thomas to distinguish him from Judas Iscariot (the Judas who identified Jesus to his arrestors and sent him to crucifixion). This Judas is the same apostle who – in the Gospel of John – is referred to as "Thomas who is called Didymos."

According to ancient Thomasian tradition, the author of the gospel had the unique position of being Jesus' twin brother. Though, in the Gospel of Thomas, this is clearly supposed to indicate a spiritual relationship; in other related pieces of Thomasian literature, such as the Book of Thomas the Contender (which was a document composed later than the Gospel of Thomas, and dug up in Nag Hammadi along with it) and the Acts of Thomas (which was also composed by the Thomasian sect and later redacted by the ancient Catholic Church fathers to be more orthodox in its teachings and placed within the New Testament Apocrypha), this relationship is supposed to be taken both spiritually and literally.

The introduction also says, "These are the *secret* sayings that the *living Jesus* spoke..." By using the word "secret" the author is telling you that these sayings are not for everyone's ears. These are the secret teachings that are only for a special "chosen" few – the solitary elect or "monachos" in Greek (which is where we get the word "Monk" from).

Furthermore, they are the "secret" teachings of the "living Jesus". The term "living Jesus" is to distinguish the dualism of the mortal man – Jesus of Nazareth – and the immortal divine being living inside him. The "living Jesus" would be a pre-existent godly being conceptually similar to the Logos in the "Gospel of John".

The theological framework for the Gospel of Thomas is determined by its cosmological outlook. The cosmology of the Gospel of Thomas is extremely dualistic. For Thomas there are only two realms of existence: the material realm and the spiritual realm. The spiritual realm is a blissful reality of goodness, life, and light; it is the Kingdom of the Father. The material realm is a reality of evil, death, and darkness. From Thomas' point of view, the material world is the world of death ruled over by the Lion (possibly a reverence to the lion-headed Yaldabaoth in classically Gnostic literature) and his minions or rulers.

While most people in this material world, according to this ancient belief, are lifeless, soulless beings (little more than animated corpses) created to serve the Lion and his rulers; a few people are actually spiritual beings in disguise. These chosen few – though clothed in a mortal body – are actually immortal pre-existent beings of light and Children of the Living Father who have become intoxicated and fallen asleep under the weight of the material world and its vices. These solitary elect, upon hearing words of the "Living Jesus", will then shake off their slumber and – upon the death of the material body – will return to the Kingdom of the Father.

In this way, the theology of Thomas is not that different from the theological concepts within the canonical Gospel of John. In fact, in most ways the Gospel of John and the Gospel of Thomas are very similar.

However, this is where the Gospel of John and the Gospel of Thomas part: while the Gospel of John clearly has a strong accent on a future eschaton in which the risen Jesus overthrows the ruler of this world, Thomas believes that the eschaton is already happening. Also, while John clearly preaches the belief in a bodily resurrection, Thomas claims that the body will never inherit life. Rather, for Thomas, the resurrection is a spiritual one.

The Hymn of the Pearl

Perhaps the best summary of the theology of the Gospel of Thomas is found in the "Hymn of the Pearl", or the "Hymn of the Apostle Thomas" – which is found within the Acts of Thomas.

In the "Hymn of the Pearl", a young prince is sent by his father in the east (East, in antiquity, was seen as symbolic of light and life) to Egypt in the west (West was seen as symbolic of death) in which lies a great pearl guarded by the dragon. The prince puts on the clothes of the Egyptians, so as not to be recognized as a foreigner. However, the dragon learns of the prince and gets the prince to eat the heavy food of the Egyptians. After eating the Egyptian food, the prince falls asleep and forgets who he is. He believes himself to be an Egyptian, when in fact he is really a prince from the East.

When the prince's Father, the king, hears of his son's capture, he sends a personified message to his son reminding him who he is and where he is from. Upon hearing the message, the prince shakes off his drunkenness, defeats the dragon, takes the pearl, removes the Egyptian clothes and returns to his home in the East.

An understanding:

The prince (a spiritual child of God) is sent by the King (his Father, God) into "the world" guarded by the dragon (the devil as understood in "the war in heaven"), in order to liberate the good souls trapped there. The prince puts on the clothes of the Egyptians (the spiritual child puts on a physical body in order to be accepted in the physical world). The prince goes "undercover" in the physical world, and follows a physical path in order to understand the ways of the physical world. In learning the ways of the complex physical world, he becomes spiritually unconscious due to the distraction of the physical path, and forgets his spiritual mission. He believes himself to be merely a physical person (susceptible to death), instead of an immortal spiritual being.

When the prince's father (God), hears of his son's capture (confusion), he reminds him of who he is and his true mission (spiritual awakening). Upon waking up spiritually, he refocuses on his spiritual path and mission, defeats the dragon (devil, denies temptation), takes the pearl (liberates the souls [rapture]), removes the Egyptian clothes (physical form of limitation) and returns home (spiritual consciousness, heaven).

The philosophy of the Gospel of Thomas

In the Thomas gospel, Jesus is a spiritual teacher, and he is offering everyone the opportunity to live (saying 4) a life that goes beyond death (saying 1), to become the ruler of their own lives (saying 2) and thus to know themselves (saying 3) and their legacy of being the children of "the living Father" (saying 3). These goals are presented in the image of "entering the Kingdom" by the methodology of insight that goes beyond duality (saying 22)

The "Gospel of Thomas" shows no concern for doctrines such as "God", "original sin", "Christ", "divinity", etc.

The Gospel of Thomas is mystical and emphasizes a direct and unmediated experience of the truth of life. In Thomas v.108, Jesus said, "Whoever drinks from my mouth will become as I am; I myself shall become that person, and the hidden things will be revealed to him." Furthermore, salvation is personal and found through spiritual (psychological) introspection. In Thomas v.70, Jesus says, "If you bring forth what is within you, what you have will save you. If you do not bring it forth, what you do not have within you will kill you". As such, this form of salvation is idiosyncratic and without literal explanation unless read from a psychological perspective related to Self vs. ego.

In Thomas v.3, Jesus says,

...the Kingdom of God is inside of you, and it is outside of you. When you come to know yourselves, then you will become known, and you will realize that it is you who are the sons of the living Father. But if you will not know yourselves, you dwell in poverty, and it is you who are that poverty.

In the other four gospels, Jesus is frequently called upon to explain the meanings of parables or the correct procedure for prayer. In Thomas v.6, his disciples asked him, "Do you want us to fast? How should we pray? Should we give to charity? What diet should we observe?" For reasons unknown, Jesus' answer is found in v.14 and he emphasizes that what is encountered in the world will not defile a person but what comes out from the mouth will. This is just one example in "Thomas" in which the hearer's attention is directed away from objectified judgments of the world to knowing oneself in direct and straightforward manner, which is sometimes called being "as a child" or "a little one" through the unification of our dualistic thinking and modes of objectification. (For example, Sayings 22 and 37) To portray the breaking down of the dualistic perspective Jesus uses the image of fire which consumes all. (See, sayings 10 and 82).

The teaching of salvation (i.e., entering the Kingdom of Heaven) that is found in "The Gospel of Thomas" is neither that of "works" nor of "grace" as the dichotomy is found in the canonical gospels, but what might be called a third way, that of insight. The overriding concern of "the Gospel of Thomas" is to find the light within in order to be a light unto the world. (See for example, Sayings 24, 26)

In contrast to the Gospel of John, where Jesus is likened to a (divine and beloved) Lord as in ruler, the Thomas gospel portrays Jesus as more the ubiquitous vehicle of mystical inspiration and enlightenment. In Thomas v.77 where Jesus said,

I am the light that shines over all things. I am everywhere. From me all came forth, and to me all return. Split a piece of wood, and I am there. Lift a stone, and you will find me there,

In many other respects, the Thomas gospel offers terse yet familiar if not identical accounts of the sayings of Jesus as seen in the synoptic gospels.

Elaine Pagels, in her book "Beyond Belief, argues that the Thomas gospel at first fell victim to the needs of the early Christian community for solidarity in the face of persecution, then to the will of the Emperor Constantine, who at the First Council of Nicaea in 325, wanted an end to the sectarian squabbling and a universal Christian creed. She goes on to point out that in spite of it being left out of the Catholic canon, being banned and sentenced to burn, many of the mystical elements have proven to reappear perennially in the works of mystics like Jacob Boehme, Teresa of Avila and Saint John of the Cross (as long as they did not deny the uniqueness and divinity of Jesus). She concludes that the Thomas gospel gives us a rare glimpse into the diversity of beliefs in the early Christian community, an alternative perspective to the Johannine gospel.

The Gospel of Thomas's importance and author

The Gospel of Thomas is regarded by many scholars as one of the most important texts in understanding early Christianity outside the New Testament. It is one of the earliest accounts of the teaching of Jesus outside of the canonical gospels, and so is considered a valuable text. It is unique in that it is ostensibly written from the point of view of Didymus Judas Thomas, one of the twelve apostles of Jesus, and claims to contain special revelations and parables made only to Thomas. It is further unique in that the gospel is no more than a collection of Jesus' sayings and parables, and contains no narrative account of his life, which is something that all four canonical gospels include.

No major Christian group accepts this gospel as canonical or authoritive. Nonetheless, it is an important work for scholars working on the Q gospel, which itself is thought to be a collection of sayings or teachings upon which later gospels are based. Although no copy of Q has ever been discovered, the fact that Thomas is similarly a 'sayings' Gospel is taken by some as indication that the early Christians did write collections of the sayings of Jesus, and thus they feel it renders the Q theory more credible.

Most scholars consider the "Gospel of Thomas" to be a Gnostic text, since it was found in a library among others, it contains Gnostic themes, and perhaps presupposes a Gnostic worldview. Others reject this interpretation, because "Thomas" lacks the full-blown mythology of Gnosticism as described by Irenaeus of Lyons (ca.185).

The Gospel of Thomas and the historical Jesus

Many modern scholars believe that the Gospel of Thomas was written independently of the New Testament, and therefore, is a useful guide to historical Jesus research. Scholars may utilize one of a number of critical tools in biblical scholarship, the criterion of multiple attestation, to help build cases for historical reliability of the sayings of Jesus. By finding those sayings in the Gospel of Thomas that overlap with Q, Mark, Matthew, Luke, John, and Paul, scholars feel such sayings represent "multiple attestations" and therefore are more likely to come from a historical Jesus than sayings that are only singly attested.

The "Gospel of Thomas has been used by Jesus Myth theorists, such as Earl Doherty and Timothy Freke, as evidence that Christianity did not originate with a historical Jesus, but as a Jewish adaptation of the Greek mystery religions. The collection of teachings attributed to Jesus; represent part of the initiation to the mysteries of their religion.

Comparison of "The Gospel of Thomas" to the New Testament

The Gospel of Thomas does not refer to Jesus as "Christ", "Lord", or "Son of Man" as the New Testament does, but simply as "Jesus". The "Gospel of Thomas" also lacks any mention of Jesus' birth, baptism, miracles, travels, death, and resurrection. However, over half of the sayings in "Thomas", are similar to sayings and parables found in the canonical gospels.

The "Gospel of Thomas does not list the canonical twelve apostles, though it does mention James the Just, who is singled out ("No matter where you are, you are to go to James the Just, for whose sake heaven and earth came into being"); Simon Peter; Matthew; Thomas, who is taken aside and receives three points of revelation; Mary; and Salome. Though here Mary Magdalene and Salome are mentioned among the twelve disciples, the canonical Gospels and "Acts" only mention men, but make a distinction between "disciples" and the inner group of twelve "apostles" – a Greek term that does not appear in Thomas – with varying lists of names making up the canonical twelve. Despite the favorable mention of James the Just, generally considered a "pro-circumcision" Christian, the "Gospel of Thomas" also dismisses circumcision:

"His disciples said to him, "Is circumcision useful or not?" He said to them, "If it were useful, their father would produce children already circumcised from their mother. Rather, the true circumcision in spirit has become profitable in every respect."

Compare Thomas 8 SV with the Bible's gospel of Matthew 13:47-50

8. And Jesus said, "The person is like a wise fisherman who cast his net into the sea and drew it up from the sea full of little fish. Among them the wise fisherman discovered a fine large fish. He threw all the little fish back into the sea, and easily chose the large fish. Anyone here with two good ears had better listen!"

Matthew 13:47-50

47 "Once again, the kingdom of heaven is like a net that was let down into the lake and caught all kinds of fish. 48 When it was full, the fishermen pulled it up on the shore. Then they sat down and collected the good fish in baskets, but threw the bad away. 49 This is how it will be at the end of the age. The angels will come and separate the wicked from the righteous 50 and throw them into the fiery furnace, where there will be weeping and gnashing of teeth."

Note that Thomas makes a distinction between large and small fish, whereas Matthew makes a distinction between good and bad fish. Furthermore, Thomas' version has only one fish remaining, whereas Matthew's version implies many good fish remaining. The manner in which each Gospel concludes the parable is instructive. Thomas' version invites the reader to draw their own conclusions as to the interpretation of the saying, whereas Matthew provides an explanation connecting the text to an apocalyptic end of the age.

Another example is the parable of the lost sheep, which is paralleled by Matthew, Luke, John, and Thomas.

This is the parable of the lost sheep in Matthew 18:12-14

12 "What do you think? If a man owns a hundred sheep, and one of them wanders away, will he not leave the ninety-nine on the hills and go to look for the one that wandered off? 13 And if he finds it, I tell you the truth, he is happier about that one sheep than about the ninety-nine that did not wander off. 14 In the same way your Father in heaven is not willing that any of these little ones should be lost."

This is the parable of the lost sheep in Luke 15:3-7

3 then Jesus told them this parable: 4 "Suppose one of you has a hundred sheep and loses one of them. Does he not leave the ninety-nine in the open country and go after the lost sheep until he finds it? 5 And when he finds it, he joyfully puts it on his shoulders 6 and goes home. Then he calls his friends and neighbors together and says, 'Rejoice with me; I have found my lost sheep.' 7 I tell you that in the same way there will be more rejoicing in heaven over one sinner who repents than over ninety-nine righteous persons who do not need to repent."

This is the parable of the lost sheep in Thomas SV

107. Jesus said, "The Kingdom is like a shepherd who had a hundred sheep. One of them, the largest, went astray. He left the ninety-nine and looked for the one until he found it. After he had toiled, he said to the sheep, I love you more than the ninety-nine."

This is the lost sheep discourse in John 10:1-18

1 "I tell you the truth, the man who does not enter the sheep pen by the gate, but climbs in by some other way, is a thief and a robber. 2 The man who enters by the gate is the shepherd of his sheep. 3 The watchman opens the gate for him, and the sheep listen to his voice. He calls his own sheep by name and leads them out. 4 When he has brought out all his own, he goes on ahead of them, and his sheep follow him because they know his voice. 5 But they will never follow a stranger; in fact they will run away from him because they do not recognize a stranger's voice." 6 Jesus used this figure of speech, but they did not understand what he was telling them. 7 Therefore Jesus said again, "I tell you the truth, I am the gate; whoever enters through me will be saved. [1] He will come in and go out, and find pasture. 10 The thief comes only to steal and kill and destroy; I have come that they may have life, and have it to the full. 11 "I am the good shepherd. The good shepherd lays down his life for the sheep. 12 The hired hand is not the shepherd who owns the sheep. So when he sees the wolf coming, he abandons the sheep and runs away. Then the wolf attacks the flock and scatters it. The man runs away because he is a hired hand and cares nothing for the sheep. "I am the good shepherd; I know my sheep and my sheep know me – 15 just as the Father knows me and I know the Father – and I lay down my life for the sheep. 16 I have other sheep that are not of this sheep pen. I must bring them also. They too will listen to my voice, and there shall be one flock and one shepherd. 17 The reason my Father loves me is that I lay down my life – only to take it up again. 18 No one takes it from me, but I lay it down of my own accord. I have authority to lay it down and authority to take it up again. This command I received from my Father."

Other parallels include

Matthew 10:16 which parallels Thomas 39.

Matthew 10:37 which parallels Thomas 55 and 101

Matthew 10:27 which parallels Thomas 33a

Matthew 10:34-36 which parallels Thomas 16

Matthew 10:26 which parallels Thomas 5b

For a simpler understanding:

This world was originally designed as a spiritual nursery. One of the Angels in charge of tending to the growing spirits turned against God and created a veil of forgetfulness which made us forget our spiritual memory. His selfish, negative energy poisoned this world which made God quarantine this world so that negativity will not escape. The negative angel lives inside of each and every one of us and has gone to great lengths to prevent us from recovering our spiritual memories, (which is what magic mushrooms do) Even though this world has been separated from the kingdom of Heaven, God has never lost hope that we will defeat the negative angel and purge this world of his influence. The "gate" which Jesus refers to, is the gate of consciousness. Throughout the levels of psychedelic experience 1-5, various tests will be faced. The level 3 test is the test of life value. If you are unwilling to relinquish your life, you will never get to level 4. The Level 4 test is the reasoning test. If you are willing to give up your life you will be tested on the reason for that willingness. If it is because you simply want to escape, you will not pass, and you will be returned. If you wish to give it up for the good of others, you will pass. Level 5 is the final test. It is simple, will you stay spiritually conscious (in heaven) or return to the unconscious world (hell) with your newly found knowledge, to serve our Father's will in order to save the others.

The easiest way to get past these tests is to keep the thought in your head, that when the fear of Death pops into your mind, it's not actually you who's dying, but instead it's the negative being inside of you who is dying. He forces you to feel his own fear of death to trick you into not letting him go, but if you can push past that fear, the spiritual medicine that the magic mushrooms contain can provide you with insights beyond that of your wildest imagination. Jesus conquered his demon, and the negative angel in the world has tried to prevent anyone else from doing as he did. But he can't stop me! This test we face is an individual test. I can only take my own test, you must take yours. I can help you prepare for your test, but ultimately, your test is your own to pass or fail. Will you let go of yourself, or not?

It's as easy as letting go of something or someone you don't really need or want any way (your ego). If you had an acquaintance, which every time you were together, bad things happened, you got in trouble, or hurt. Would you still choose to stay their friend? Probably not!

It's as easy as choosing to be happy or unhappy. So just let it all go....

The most important thing to understand is that Jesus was a profoundly spiritual mystic. We can all be like him by realizing the truth, eating the manna, and understanding the similarities between Mysticism (specifically "the five stages of the universal mystic way"), the psychedelic experience (specifically "The five levels"), the near death experience (specifically "the five levels"), and the Gospel of Thomas.

The Similarities Are Undeniable

The five stages of the universal mystic path:

The Mystical Perspective

Process Author and mystic, Evelyn Underhill (*Name "Underhill" is referenced in "Lord of the rings"*) outlines the "universal mystic way", the actual process by which the mystic arrives at union with the absolute. She identifies "five stages of this process". (*It is no coincidence that there are also five levels of the "psychedelic experience", because this is also linked to the "Forbidden fruit" a.k.a. "Fruit of Knowledge"*)

1) First is the "awakening", the stage in which one begins to have some "consciousness of absolute or divine reality" (*spiritual consciousness*)

2) The second stage is one of "purgation" which is characterized by an "awareness of one's own imperfections and finiteness". The response in this stage is one of self-discipline (*self-control*) and mortification.

3) The third stage "illumination", is reached by artists and visionaries as well as being the final stage of some mystics. It is marked by a consciousness of a transcendental order and a "vision of a new heaven" and a "new earth".

4) The great mystics go beyond the stage of illumination to a fourth stage which Underhill, borrowing the language of St. John of the cross, calls "The dark night of the soul". This stage, only experienced by the few, is one of final and complete purification and is marked by confusion, helplessness, stagnation of the will, and a sense of the withdrawal of God's presence. It is the period of final "unselfing" and the surrender to the hidden purposes of the divine will.

5) The final and last stage is one of "union with the object of love, the one Reality, God". Here the self has been permanently established on a transcendental level and liberated for a new purpose. Filled up with the Divine Will, it immerses itself in the temporal order (*the temporary physical world*), the world of "appearances" in order to incarnate the eternal in time (*time being a manifestation of the physical mind*), to become the mediator between humanity and eternity. (In order to be the messenger of God)

(*Our physical lives go by in an instant against the scope of eternity, as if our entire physical lives are simply a dream being had by our true eternal spiritual form, the problem is that we do not realize we're asleep, and therefore do not know how to wake up.*)

Five levels of psychedelic experience:

Levels of psychedelic experience

The Psychedelic Experience FAQ

(http://www.erowid.org/psychoactives/faqs/psychedelic_experience_faq.shtml) describes five different levels of psychedelic experience acquired by substances and chemicals:

Level 1

This level produces a mild "high" effect, with some visual enhancement (e.g. brighter colors) and music sounds "wider", or more piercing to the ears. There is a sense that one's thoughts are spiraling into themselves. This level can be achieved from a normal dose of cannabis or a very low dose of a classic psychedelic such as psilocybin. Occasionally common prescription drugs like SSRIs can produce mild "trippy" effects, as well, through they are not normally classified as psychedelic experiences because they are so mild.

Level 2

Bright colors; visuals (e.g. things like walls and ceilings may appear to move or breath); some two-dimensional patterns become apparent upon shutting eyes. Confused, cyclic (thought loop) or reminiscent thoughts. Déjà vu is commonly reported. Change in short term memory leads to continually distracting thought patterns. While it may become increasingly difficult to follow a single train of thought, at other times one might find themselves lost in deep introspection about one specific idea or problem. The need to see 'normal' reality becomes less, the urge to venture 'beyond the void' becomes more. Level 3 tripping can intersperse with level 2 as long as eyes are shut. This state can be achieved from higher doses of cannabis or a low dose of psilocybin or LSD.

Level 3

Very obvious visuals, everything looking curved and/or warped, patterns, kaleidoscopes or fractal images seen on walls, landscapes, faces, etc. Closed eye hallucinations become three dimensional. There is some confusing of the senses (synesthesia). Time distortions and "moments of eternity". Movement at times becomes extremely difficult. A normal dose of either psilocybin or LSD can produce this state.

Level 4

Strong visual effects (e.g. objects morphing into other objects). Dissolving or multiple splitting of the ego (e.g. things start talking, "burning bush", or feeling of contradictory things simultaneously). The loss of sense of self can bring a shift in the sense of reality, often accompanied by a sense of ineffable lucidity (abstract clarity, and understanding of subjects not usually thought about, but difficult to find words capable of explaining). Time becomes very distorted and participants may perceive an activity lasting only minutes to have encompassed hours of their own reality (or vice versa) (similar to seeing your whole life flashing before you in the last moment before you "die"). Out-of-body experiences and mystical visions are common at this level. A high dose of psilocybin or LSD can produce this effect, as can a normal dose of Salvia divinorum.

Level 5

Total loss of visual connection with reality (Similar to The Matrix, or a complete spiritual awakening). The senses cease to function in the normal way. One may feel like they are merging with space, other objects, or the universe, or feel oneness with the world. There are powerful, and sometimes brutal, psycho-physical reactions interpreted by some users as reliving their own birth. Feelings of reaching to the beginning or the end of space and time can be experienced. The loss of reality becomes so extreme that it becomes ineffable (understood but impossible to relate in words). Dream or movie-like states, people have reported seeing themselves in entirely different settings than their original setting.

Many people experience religious phenomenon at this level. Often mentioned are an "all-powerful presence" or a "universal knowledge", which many equate to their idea of God or enlightenment.

Earlier levels are relatively easy to describe in terms of measureable changes in perception and thought patterns. "Ego loss", or complete dissolution of one's awareness of the existence of Self, (the separation of your spiritual self, from your physical self) is an essential trait of level 5 experiences; the boundaries between "self" and encompassing reality cease to exist, and all that one is conscious of, is the abstract manifestations of the hallucination (the spirit world). Thoughts are not processed or realized in words or an "inner voice", as in everyday life; in the midst of a level 5 hallucination, it is essentially impossible to distinguish conscious thought from the hallucination itself. This feeling has been described, with Tryptamine-based hallucinogens like LSD or high doses of psilocybin, as a sense of "oneness" with the universe; with extremely powerful entheogens such as DMT or salvia divinorum, the resultant hallucination is difficult to describe, but has been likened by some to being "transformed into a Picasso painting".

Many people claim to have spoken to intelligent entities during their trips, to have experienced alternate dimensions (the spirit world), or to have existed for thousands of years (in spirit form on the plane of eternity) - often not as a human but as an abstract entity such as shadow or paint-though the trip itself, in the case of salvia and DMT, "the trip" lasted only five to ten minutes. This effect can be produced in high doses of LSD, Ketamine, salvia divinorum, and high doses of psilocybin. DMT is known to send people to level 5 with an average dose, making it one of the most potent and psychoactive psychedelics known to man.

The near death experience: (five levels)

Kenneth Ring (1980) subdivided the NDE on a 5 stage continuum:

Stage 1: Feelings of peace and contentment

Stage 2: A sense of detachment from the body

Stage 3: entering a transitional world of darkness (rapid movement through a long dark tunnel: "the tunnel experience")

Stage 4: Emerging into bright light

Stage 5: Entering the light

Ring stated, however, that 60% experienced stage 1, but only 10% experienced stage 5.

The Meaning Of "Life":

I can tell you why we are "here", but I cannot make you believe or understand why, that is up to you. Ok, here we go. Our lives are a test. In the beginning, before "humans" came to being in this place, there were spiritual beings. These spiritual beings were given a choice. That choice was to be servants of our spiritual father and do what they were told, or to turn away from our spiritual father and have a (supposedly better) physical life in which they could do whatever they wanted. The eternal spirits that gave into the temptation to have the physical life fell unconscious. What they were not told was that they were actually choosing to live or die, because death is simply "The loss of conscious thought". We are the offspring of those unconscious spirits. As we are born into the unconscious world, we are also faced with the same choice (test) as they were. This test lies before us every second of every day of our "physical" lives. There is no cheating in this test. There is no easy way around it. We must all commit ourselves to our decision 100% (no looking back). Here is the choice: Will you have a physical life (will you enjoy dying)? Or will you surrender your "physical" life (death) to attain your spiritual consciousness (life)? This is why Jesus willingly went to his own crucifixion. He understood this choice because he indeed, ate "the fruit of knowledge" and had his own "level 5" psychedelic experience.

To further your own understanding:

1. Learn to grow pure psilocybin mushrooms, use the internet to find "The magic mushroom growers guide". Grow some. Prepare yourself by "fasting" for 1-3 days (as the ancient mystics did), then eat the mushrooms, following the dosage recommendations.
2. After your "experience" use the internet "Wikipedia" to research: Mysticism, Jesus, Manna, Psilocybin, Psilocybin mushrooms, Psychedelic experience, Near Death experience, The Mormon "Plan of Salvation", Reincarnation, Buddhism, Eschatology, Hell, Final Judgment, The War in Heaven, Consciousness, Reality, and Catharism. That's just for starters....
3. Don't dismiss your experience. Focus and reflect on it....

Or you could just buy my other book... The Big Picture- making sense out of life and religion, by Sean Williams. Thanks for reading this one....Sean

"I do not feel obliged to believe that the same God who has endowed us with sense, reason, and intellect has intended us to forgo their use"...Galileo Galilei

"The earth is the cradle of the mind, but one cannot eternally live in a cradle" Konstantine Tsiolkovsky

"Every surfer understands. You'll never ride that great wave, if you're afraid to drop in. Commitment is the key." Sean Williams

Enlightenment is an understanding of your true "self" and your spiritual condition. Sean Williams

Against the scope of eternity, our entire physical lives go by in a moment. So if we actually do have a "life flashing before our eyes moment" before we physically die, can it not be understood that our entire physical lives are actually that moment? Who's to say that we aren't all already dead and simply watching our lives in retrospect? Would experiencing every thought, every decision, every second of every day, during our judgment, not be exactly like "living"? Hmmmmn. What if all we really need to learn how to do is just let go? Sean Williams

The true illusion is right before our eyes, every second of every day, and yet most people will never realize it. It is the illusion that we are actually "alive". Sean Williams

At the moment of my physical birth, I died. Once I surrender my physical life to God, upon my physical death, I will regain life once more. Death is simply the loss of conscious thought. Spiritual consciousness and physical consciousness are two different things; in order for one to begin, one has to end, because one cannot be in two places at the same time. Sean Williams

The original "fallen" angels simply fell unconscious. To free someone from an unconscious condition, can also be understood as "resurrecting" them. I have been sent to give you the power to free yourself, for knowledge truly is power. I cannot free you; the same as I cannot die for your sins, but you can surrender your own physical life and return to spiritual consciousness. The desire to have a physical life is the original sin (temptation) after all, which we must all repent, and only by understanding that, and surrendering that desire will we be allowed to "wake up". Sean Williams

Prayers for physical things will never be answered. God will and wants to give spiritual gifts though (knowledge). We must all understand that he will not give those gifts to those of us who are un-worthy. So how do we prove ourselves worthy to God? We prove ourselves worthy through the surrendering of our physical lives to him and his will. This is what magic mushrooms do. They give us the opportunity to prove ourselves before God. They test our resolve and prove without a doubt how far we as individuals are willing to go. Would you give up "your" physical life for God? Sean Williams

This is your "wake-up" call..... God wants all of his unconscious children to wake up, he misses us.....this is his plan... Sean Williams

www.ingramcontent.com/pod-product-compliance
Lightning Source LLC
LaVergne TN
LVHW070144110826
845147LV00002B/322

* 9 7 8 0 5 7 8 0 2 0 7 2 3 *